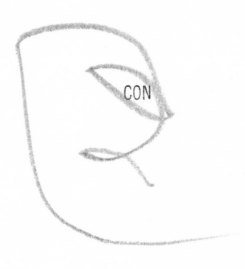

MILLIONAIRE
BY THIRTY

Also by Douglas R. Andrew

Missed Fortune

Missed Fortune 101

The Last Chance Millionaire

MILLIONAIRE BY THIRTY

The Quickest Path to Early Financial Independence

DOUGLAS R. ANDREW,

EMRON D. ANDREW,

AND

AARON R. ANDREW

BUSINESS PLUS

NEW YORK   BOSTON

The materials in this book represent the opinions of the authors and may not be applicable to all situations. Due to the frequency of changing laws and regulations, some aspects of this work may be out of date, even upon first publication. Accordingly, the authors and publisher assume no responsibility for actions taken by readers based upon the advice offered in this book. You should use caution in applying the material contained in this book to your specific situation and should seek competent advice from a qualified professional. Please provide your comments directly to the authors.

Business Plus
Hachette Book Group USA
237 Park Avenue
New York, NY 10017
Visit our Web site at www.HachetteBookGroupUSA.com.

Business Plus is an imprint of Grand Central Publishing.
The Business Plus name and logo are trademarks of Hachette Book Group USA, Inc.

Printed in the United States of America

First Edition: April 2008

10 9 8 7 6 5 4 3 2 1

Library of Congress Cataloging-in-Publication Data

Andrew, Douglas R.
   Millionaire by thirty : the quickest path to early financial independence / Douglas R. Andrew, Emron D. Andrew, and Aaron R. Andrew.—1st ed.
      p. cm.
   Includes index.
   ISBN-13: 978-0-446-50184-2
   ISBN-10: 0-446-50184-0
   1. Finance, Personal—Handbooks, manuals, etc. I. Andrew, Emron D. II. Andrew, Aaron R. III. Title.

   HG179.A55984 2008
   332.024'01—dc22

                                                        2007043669

To our Family and Posterity:

May the principles and insights
Contained in this book
Bring you
Clarity, Balance, Focus, and Confidence
To help you accomplish
Your Greatest Dreams
And create a
Meaningful Transformation
In your lives

Contents

Authors' Note

Are you ready for something different? Are you tired of reading the same-old, same-old financial advice? Are you hungry for newer, proven strategies that can propel you far ahead, giving you the opportunity to achieve an abundant life while you're still young?

This book is not like other personal finance books out there:

- It does not instruct you to cut up your credit cards in a race to be debt-free. Why? Because being totally debt-free can actually *cost* you money.
- It does not encourage you to send in extra principal payments against your mortgage. Why? Because your mortgage can be one of your biggest friends in achieving wealth.
- It does not discourage you by suggesting ideas like socking away the cost of a latte a day for forty years to become a millionaire. Why? Because there are much better ways to speed along the path to financial freedom.

Rather, this book can help you know how to generate wealth quickly and safely by using proven strategies:

- This book will teach you how to become your own banker and amass a tremendous fortune by using preferred debt to conserve and safely build your net worth to more than $1 million.

- This book will show you how to become a "Thriver"— having your money generating more than you do by working at your job—within ten years.
- It will take conflicting information you are bombarded with and filter it so you can separate myth from reality.
- It contains fresh, new, and different approaches to managing debt and using safe, positive leverage to attain a million-dollar net worth within ten years.

Millionaire by Thirty is NOT the older generation's book of how to become wealthy. Chances are, your parents don't even know about these strategies; but if they had known, they would be far better off today.

Welcome to the exciting, best way to financial independence.

—Doug, Emron, and Aaron Andrew

Preface

You are about to embark on a wonderful journey that leads to financial freedom. It is an exciting trip—and the best part is that you do not have to wait until you are in your forties, fifties, or older. You can take the first strides now, in your teens or early twenties, and be well on the way toward millionaire status by the time you reach your early thirties.

You'll note that there are three authors involved. For more than thirty years as a financial strategist, I, Douglas R. Andrew, have helped many clients of all ages become wealthy by using proven strategies that I have developed. Two of my finest students have been my sons, Emron and Aaron, who are both now in their twenties. They have learned and applied the concepts I have outlined in my earlier books, *Missed Fortune, Missed Fortune 101*, and *The Last Chance Millionaire*, and the result is that they are far ahead of most of their peers in understanding the keys to financial success.

In recent years, Emron and Aaron have joined my firm, and they now have clients nationwide whom they advise for asset optimization, equity management, and wealth empowerment. They are part of my instructional staff, which teaches advanced curriculum monthly at the Missed Fortune University™. They have written and designed sophisticated asset optimization software used by hundreds of financial advisors nationwide.

Emron and Aaron have absorbed life lessons, principles of ethical behavior, and the concept of Quadrant Living, which we will soon explain, from my wife, Sharee, and I. (I have been lucky enough to be married to Sharee for thirty-four years, and I give her so much credit for the love and happiness we all share in the family.) What I am most proud of is that our sons are living, personal examples of the Missed Fortune™ concepts. Starting out in life, they were not given anything except a proper education. Beginning from scratch with relatively no financial assets and initial incomes of $30,000 a year at the age of twenty-two, they have used the ideas in this book to each accumulate a net worth that now exceeds $1 million.

Does that sound like an unattainable goal to you? Emron, Aaron, and I have recognized that most young adults do not grow up in families that discuss financial independence at the dinner table. Many of you are bright and eager to learn—yet you don't know where the starting line toward fiscal responsibility and wealth is, much less how long or difficult the path may be.

We know that as you begin your earning years, particularly after college, you often have high hopes. But you may have become distracted by your social life, your career, or your friends. You may wish for financial security but don't possess the basic knowledge of budgets, savings, or credit to lead you there. You may grow disenchanted as you try to hit the curveballs life may throw at you.

Some of you may feel lost because your parents have always had to struggle to make ends meet. Some of you may have parents who want to give you money rather than teach you how to conserve and maximize it. And still others of you may have grown up surrounded by examples of how wealth is used to buy material goods, while spiritual and civic assets are left by the wayside.

That is why we begin by assuming that your vision of the future may be a little blurry. You may feel anxious and confused about such issues as student loans and credit cards. You may not be able to think beyond your next paycheck because you must meet payments for an apartment and a car.

This book is intended to show you how our ideas can bring your financial picture into clear focus. In the forthcoming chapters, we show you how to:

- Manage finances
- Build good credit
- Buy your first house
- Save and invest safely
- Understand and avoid unnecessary taxes
- Identify which employer-offered savings plans are best to participate in

We intend to give you a fresh, contrarian approach to managing debt and to using safe, positive leverage to attain a million-dollar net worth within ten years. The interest earnings on your nest egg will be sufficient enough by age thirty to meet your basic living expenses, and by your mid-thirties your investments can be generating more income than you do by working.

This book will take conflicting information you are bombarded with and filter it so you can separate myth from reality. We have tried not to overwhelm you with too many charts, tables, or calculations. For those who wish to dig more deeply into this mine of information, or see the mathematical proof of the conclusions that we draw, we have provided a Web portal where you can find more details on some of the more complex issues in each chapter.

The Missed Fortune™ concepts have made Emron's and Aaron's lives abundant, not just in dollars, but also in discipline, in love, and in charity. They are responsible, accountable young men who have much to offer their own families and their community in future years. If you are looking for ideas, believe us, you will find them here. If you are merely looking for schemes or scams, please go elsewhere. Above all, we are believers in balance, not only checkbook balance, but a balance of life and work.

Step by step, we are going to show you that you can grow your wealth and become confident in your ability to provide for yourself and your loved ones. Perhaps most important—certainly more important than fiscal wealth—is the sense of *self-worth* you will feel when you discover that it is possible to "touch all the bases," to manage your core assets, your experience, your contributions, and your finances, and to create harmony in your life each and every day. We invite you to join us in this great voyage. It begins right now, so turn the page and let's get under way.

MILLIONAIRE BY THIRTY

CHAPTER 1

Wake Up and Step Out of the Financial Darkness

Stop Feeling Confused, Isolated, and Powerless About Your Finances

DO YOU FEEL LIKE YOU'RE IN A fog when it comes to your finances?

Awhile back when we were visiting San Francisco, we woke up to one of the murkiest fogs we had ever seen. We had been hoping to enjoy the view of the bay from our downtown hotel, but the mists were so thick, we were lucky to see down the street. By afternoon, however, something wonderful happened. The fog had lifted, and we could see the deep blue bay shining in the sunlight.

In the same way, many young men and women in their early twenties who are smart, capable, and well-educated may not have clarity about their financial vision until they reach their thirties or forties.

This book is designed to help lift that fog right now so you can see your way clearly—so you can buy your first house, start accumulating assets, and get past the mist that clouds your financial future.

You don't have to wait thirty years—with the principles this book teaches, you can be on your way toward a net worth of $1 million by the time you are in your thirties.

My sons, Emron and Aaron, have applied these principles in their twenties and are already seeing success. As explained in the preface, they have learned these powerful strategies from myself and my wonderful wife of thirty-four years, Sharee. They now have clients nationwide whom they advise for asset optimization, equity management, and wealth empowerment. They are part of my instructional staff, which teaches advanced curriculum monthly at the Missed Fortune University™. They have written and designed sophisticated asset optimization software used by hundreds of financial advisors nationwide.

My sons are living, personal examples of the Missed Fortune™ concepts. They have not been given anything except the proper education. Starting from scratch with relatively no financial assets and beginning incomes of $30,000 a year at the age of twenty-two, they have used the strategies that will be disclosed in this book to each accumulate assets totaling more than $1.5 million by the ages of twenty-six (Aaron) and twenty-eight (Emron). And their individual financial net worth (the worth of everything they own minus what they owe) just surpassed the $1 million mark.

In addition to their active income from monthly earnings, they each enjoy passive income in excess of $3,500 a month and portfolio income in excess of $1,000 per month from their personal investments. Their assets are increasing in value about $70,000 per year. By age thirty, their *money at work* should be earning more than they *do at work*.

As you are about to see, throughout this book I offer my "fatherly advice" to readers, just as I did to my sons. In addition Emron and Aaron will speak directly to you, often using insights from their own experiences to demonstrate how you can accomplish similar dynamic results with your own money. Together we'll take real-world examples drawn from Emron, Aaron, and their friends* to illustrate how you, too, can stop feeling confused, isolated, or powerless about wealth.

What Obstacles Are Facing You as You Start Out?

One time Emron was talking to his friend Michael about money. He could tell Michael wasn't quite following along, even though they weren't discussing anything too deep—just the basics of personal finance like budgeting, savings, credit cards, debt, and home buying. But then Emron realized it wasn't entirely Michael's fault.

There was a good reason why Michael didn't have a grasp of the fundamentals. While many American high schools offer advanced calculus and honors classes in various subjects, very few give students a chance to learn simple financial literacy. In fact, only fourteen states require schools to offer a consumer education program that includes personal finance. Not surprisingly, the result is that, according to one report, "high school seniors' basic financial literacy is declining."†

Meanwhile, young people don't get enough practical training at home—the same report says 30 percent "rarely or never discuss saving and investing" with their parents. Even those who do may think that their parents, the Baby Boomers, are out of step with the financial realities of today compared with their own early adulthood. And as I wrote in my book *The Last Chance Millionaire*, Boomers themselves have made numerous blunders in managing their money. Is it any wonder that you lack self-confidence in dealing with money, or feel financially illiterate, despite your education?

We're not talking about a small group. There are approximately 100 million Americans between the ages of sixteen and thirty-five.

---

* We have changed their names to protect their privacy and in some cases created composite examples based on several people.
† Studies by the National Endowment for Financial Education, http://www.exten sion.umn.edu/youth&money/.

You are entering or have just recently entered the workforce. You are learning how to earn an income, yet you may be among the many who do not know how to save or accumulate wealth. You lack both knowledge and confidence to move ahead. The average net worth of an individual under age thirty-five is approximately $15,000. If home equity is excluded from that, the average is less than $5,000.

Is it any wonder that seven out of ten young adults polled recently said they don't earn enough to lead the kind of life they want to lead? Or that almost seven in ten say that growing rich is their most important goal in life?*

The world you're maturing in can be a scary place. "Even before the events of 9/11, terrorism had already become a national phenomenon in the 90s with the Oklahoma City, World Trade Center, and Atlanta Summer Olympics bombings. School shootings in suburban and rural America exacerbated the fears," summarizes one study of this group, which is often called "Generation Y" or "Generation Next." "Designer drugs, violence-packed video games, sexually charged advertising, TV, music, and movies bombarded their everyday lives and still do."†

Nevertheless, young adults today have enough of their own special skills to make Boomers envious. They are more mobile than most of their parents were, more willing to take risks, more interested in global social issues, and more comfortable with technology—as any parents whose children have fixed their computers and set up their entertainment centers can tell you.

Whether you are either deeply worried or not worried enough about your financial situation, you are likely aware there are plenty of tools available to deal with money; it's a question of choosing the best ones and learning how to use them.

---

* "A Portrait of "Generation Next," Pew Research Center, Jan. 9, 2007.
† from http://www.rainmakerthinking.com/mix2007.doc.

Can You Identify with These Feelings?

Are you *confused* because, despite a college education, you believe you are financially illiterate?

Do you feel *trapped* because of the way your parents brought you up to think about money?

Are you *hesitant* to make long-term decisions about money or employers?

Are you *fearful* that there will always be too much month left at the end of your money?

That's why we've written this book. We want you to consider it as the starter's guide to understanding basic concepts and strategies in order to attain financial security early in life.

Are You Feeling Confused about Your Finances?

Even if you have had a good high school and/or college education, you may be confused when faced with everyday money matters. Many young people feel they are trapped in circumstances caused by their family, upbringing, or environment.

Emron's friend Adam felt he would always be held down by his family's blue-collar mentality. He graduated from college and got a job teaching English at a high school in Denver, but he believed he would never be able to climb the salary ladder or reach a better standard of living than his parents. After Adam got married and his wife was expecting a baby, he was still afraid to listen to Emron's advice. "We need more money to do what you're telling us to do," said Adam.

Another friend, Joshua, was also confused about finances, even though his background was the opposite of Adam's. Joshua came from a wealthy family and was studying to be a lawyer, like his father. But he had no sense of how to establish his own credit or how to live within his means. While he was attending law school, Josh's parents paid the rent on a small apartment and handed Josh a handsome monthly allowance. "It's just until I get a job and start

earning big bucks," he said. Joshua would use money from his allowance to pay credit card debt on his latest toys, such as a giant
plasma-screen TV.

Often parents are understandably so eager to help their children
that they may inadvertently hurt them. While parents' generosity is
well-intentioned, it's what I call "giving your kids a fish instead of
teaching them *how* to fish." College is an ideal time to begin learning how to earn and put money to work, rather than just studying
and playing.

Do You Feel Powerless about Your Finances?

We know that debt hangs over the heads of many young adults
just like that San Francisco fog. Studies indicate that nearly two-
thirds graduate from college with thousands of dollars owed in student loans. One of our key convictions is that debt is not always
bad—in fact, certain kinds of debt can be your friend, not your foe.
It's what *kind* of debt you have, and *how* you handle it.

As they start their working lives, too many young adults think
they must pay off their student loans before they do anything else.
Some are so concerned about those loans that they make the wrong
choices. In a recent *USA Today* survey, 22 percent said they accepted
a "job they otherwise wouldn't have because they needed more
money to pay off student-loan debt"; 29 percent put off or chose
"not to pursue more education"; 26 percent have put off buying a
home. And a smaller percentage even postponed marriage and having kids.[*]

That's like driving a car with the parking brake on. With a "pay
off every loan as fast as you can" mentality, you wind up struggling
to make ends meet—unless someone teaches you the secrets of debt
management.

We are about to show you:

---

[*] Mindy Fetterman and Barbara Hansen, "Young People Struggle to Deal with Kiss of
Debt," USAtoday.com, Nov. 20, 2006.

- How to create true net worth, using assets as well as liabilities
- How to look at debt in a new, enlightened way
- What kind of debt costs you dearly, versus debt that actually helps your money grow
- How you can get ahead, regardless of your loans

Perhaps like many young adults, the threat of being in debt hangs over your head like a sword. You may feel powerless to do anything about where you dwell besides rent, because you don't know how to buy a house. Maybe you wonder how you will ever save enough for a down payment. It's possible the idea of a mortgage seems more than you can handle. A big part of our task in this book is to clear up this haze of myths and misconceptions so you can see how sunny this early part of your adult life can be.

Do You Feel Isolated?

The transition from the "learning years" to the "earning years" may not always be easy. Once young adults enter the workforce, they may still feel broke all the time. They have many doubts about how to manage a paycheck. Perhaps you feel that your first job, which only pays you $30,000 to $40,000 a year, is too meager to let you accumulate much. (The median income for families headed by people aged twenty to twenty-nine was just under $28,000 in 2004, according to Federal Reserve statistics.)

Then you feel futile as you watch a big chunk of your paycheck going to pay rent on your first apartment. I'm sure you know peers who have become members of the "boomerang" generation by moving back home with their Baby Boomer parents.

Ryan, a friend of Aaron's, lived with his parents in Irvine, California, while he was getting his MBA in finance. Then he got married, and he and his bride moved into a small student housing apartment near campus. Once he had his advanced degree, he got a good entry-level job with a firm in Irvine. The young couple finally rented their own place, but it wasn't cheap. They paid $1,200 a month in rent. Dad was always accommodating—he gave Ryan a check every month to cover part of the rent.

Aaron wished his friends could feel more independent and "in motion" about their finances. So he explained that Ryan could just as easily find a house in a less expensive but nice area, and that he could put that same $1,200 into house payments—a move that would help his current financial picture and perhaps brighten the future, since just a small increase in home prices would boost his equity. Aaron pointed out that it really was possible, since he had already bought his own house and was even building a $250,000 cabin with Emron.

Ryan's dad, who like most Boomers had only heard of conventional financial planning strategies, was skeptical. He warned Aaron that he would end up being up to his eyeballs in debt and cautioned him against being irresponsible.

That was two years ago. Today, Ryan is still tossing his $1,200 down the "black hole" known as rent each month (which earns him nothing). He has bought a snazzy used Mustang for himself and is shelling out $300 a month on his car loan, which is not tax-deductible.

Contrast that to Aaron, who followed unconventional but proven strategies. With a home and a cabin that have both gone up in value, he has been able to add $200,000 to his net worth, thanks to appreciation in the two properties. And he benefits from one of the best tax deductions this country has to offer: home mortgage interest.

Ryan's dad is no longer worried about Aaron. In fact, he's said he's pretty amazed.

Are You Ready to Hear Some Powerful Advice?

In this book we will boil down complex financial issues by using a powerful method of teaching concepts grouped in threes. The lesson you can learn from Ryan's story? That there are three kinds of people in the world:

1) People who *make* things happen
2) People who *watch* things happen
3) People who *wonder* what happened

In this chapter, we have outlined why young people often feel:

1) Confused
2) Isolated
3) Powerless

At this point, you might ask yourself, "Am I too proud to ask for advice about money?" Or do you figure you'll watch your friends—the blind leading the blind—and just "try to keep up with the Joneses"?

That's like trying to drive with your car stuck in neutral. Your foot is on the gas, but you don't seem to be going anywhere. This book will help you get moving:

- We are about to teach you that even if you are just starting out in life, you can make your money earn as much as you do.
- We will guide you in managing your income, controlling your debts, and buying your first house.
- This book will teach you how to save and invest safely, without risking your own money, using what we call the three marvels of wealth accumulation.
- Once you understand these three concepts, you'll be able to shift into a higher gear, put your paycheck to work

for you instead of your landlord, and buy your first house . . . and then your second.

- We'll also show you how to understand and avoid unnecessary taxes, and identify which employer-offered savings plans are best to participate in.
- We will show you how to put your finances on cruise control—how to find money and create more money by using the strategies explained in the Missed Fortune book series—so you don't miss out on your fortune early in life.

Are You Willing to Learn a New Approach to Wealth?

With the help of this book, you can gain the crucial knowledge you need to manage your money, build good credit, and get a proper mortgage. We can teach you how to put money into safe investments, save money in a tax-favored environment, and create a retirement plan that makes you rich—not Uncle Sam.

It will give a fresh, contrarian approach to managing debt and using safe, positive leverage to attain a million-dollar net worth within as short as ten years. If you start as early as age twenty-two, the interest earnings on your nest egg can be sufficient enough by age thirty to meet your basic living expenses, and by age thirty-two your investments can be generating more income than you do by working. *This book will take conflicting information you are bombarded with and filter it so you can separate myth from reality.*

Are You Able to Take the Challenge?

Ours is not the same-old, same-old tired financial advice. We won't discourage you by suggesting that you sock away five dollars a day for forty years. And we're not going to bury you in charts and tables and worksheets. We will try to keep this simple so you can get a solid grip on the principles without losing them in a forest of calculations. Please realize, however, that this book is not for "idiots," nor do we consider you "dummies." We recognize that you are adults and can jot down numbers when necessary.

We *do* ask that, for now, you accept our ground rules:

1) Keep an open mind about our strategies, even if some sound very different from the ones your parents or others have followed.
2) Listen to our arguments all the way through because they may come as a huge change from the often-repeated clichés financial advisors talk about on radio and TV.
3) Have faith that by the time you come to the last chapter, you will understand how you can look forward to a future of wealth.

In return, we promise to honor you and your peers as smart, vibrant, entrepreneurial young people who have three hundred horses under that hood and are on the brink of zooming down the highway of life. We don't want you to miss the exit ramp that leads to lifelong wealth, even if you don't have the job, home, or spouse of your dreams yet. This book will help you avoid continuing down the same old highway and direct you to the exit ramp that leads to lifelong wealth and financial independence. Even if you feel you've missed out or made mistakes, you can take the next exit, flip a U-turn, and go back to the junction where the highway leads to a thriving future of financial independence.

No matter what you have done until now, you can find the ramp marked "Financial Independence." It is great to be young and open to change. Now's the perfect time to readjust your attitude, leave your worries about debt back in the parking lot, and commit to turning in the right direction.

Our advice will help you whether you are currently attending college, just graduating from college, are a newlywed, or are still

Take the exit ramp marked "Financial Independence"
and find new direction, confidence and capability for you too!

single. In fact, this could also be a great handbook for parents who want to teach their children responsibility and accountability for the proper management of money and other resources.

Start your engines, and get ready to be empowered with the knowledge to become a millionaire by your thirties.

REMEMBER THIS

- Most people in their thirties only have a net worth of $15,000; but you *can* attain a net worth of $1 million in as little as ten years or less.
- By your mid-thirties, you can have your money generating more income than you do by working.
- Don't let your lack of knowledge stand in the way of fresh financial advice—be open to new and contrarian ideas about money.
- This book will take conflicting information you are bombarded with and filter it so you can separate myth from reality.
- This book will give you new direction to clear up confusion about money. It will give you new hope and confidence so you will not feel isolated. And it will empower you with new capability so you will not feel powerless.
- Understand that not all debt is bad—preferred debt can make you wealthy.

LEARNING LINKS

- As a token of appreciation for investing in the purchase of this book, we invite you to listen to a special audio CD entitled *Secrets of Wealthy People*. Please go to www.Missed Fortune.com/Millionaire-By-Thirty and click on the learning portal for chapter 1 to hear this enlightening information.

CHAPTER 2

Mapping Your Future

Ten Years to Financial Independence by Avoiding the Top Ten Dangers

IN 1996, TWO STANFORD UNIVERSITY graduate students in their twenties, Larry Page and Sergei Brin, started working together on creating an Internet search engine that would be all-encompassing, fast, and accurate. Within ten years, the product they developed became the world's leading Internet company, had thousands of employees, earned millions of dollars each month, and made both of them billionaires. It's called Google.

Where would you like to be in ten years? Do you feel motivated to achieve great things in your career, your financial life, and your personal life? Have you developed a strategy to stay fit and healthy, to feel personally secure, and to become financially independent no matter what curveballs life, the economy, or the job market might throw you?

Or are you just sitting back, content to be carried along by the tides of chance, hoping to get lucky?

We can't give you step-by-step instructions for creating a great Internet search engine, but we can explain the steps you need to develop a personal financial engine that will help you save and accumulate wealth. One keyword we use in talking about a financially secure future is *ownership*. It's important to commit yourself to a prudent course, take ownership of your money, and then stay on it. Other keywords? Search for ways to be *accountable* in your own life, and you'll be able to design a profitable and stable financial plan that grows as you do. Search for *strategies* that allow you to *optimize* your earnings and plan for a retirement that is not dependent on your parents, your employer, or the government.

If you aspire to become wealthy, you need to begin living in the proactive zone of *predictable results*. You need to have a vision, to cultivate an attitude that guarantees you can accomplish it, and to bypass the dangers that can derail it. You need to accept *responsibility* for your own future.

Your Keywords for the Next Decade

Jennifer: I'm ready to take ownership and be responsible, but how exactly do I develop a vision for my progress in the next decade? When you asked at our high school reunion what I think about my career and financial future, I didn't know how to answer.

Aaron: It's probably a good idea to just keep things simple. When I look ahead, I think about simplifying my vision and my goals, and I write them down. It's also helps to keep a list of keywords to set goals you can reach.

Like Aaron's former classmate Jennifer, you might be asking at this point where you should start out. We like to group things in threes, because that lets us set concise priorities for what we want to achieve. Here are keywords that work for us:

Money Keywords

- A *budget* so I can live within my means and become financially savvy
- *Multiple income streams*
- *Liquid savings* (money I can access readily) of several thousand dollars

Strategy Keywords

- Understand which kind of *debt* works for me instead of against me
- Own at least two or three *real estate properties*
- Have a *systematic roadmap* to reach financial independence in my thirties

Personal Keywords

- Be in a happy *relationship* so I can start a family when I'm ready
- Know what my unique, marketable *abilities* are
- Develop a lifetime learning commitment (LLC) for *ongoing education*

Social and *Community* Keywords

- Have *balance* in my life and work
- Belong to an *organization* or attend something of meaning
- Contribute and give back to *society*

A Map for Navigating the World of Wealth

When you are driving in an unfamiliar area, you need a good map. In the same way, to navigate the territory of wealth through the next decade, you need a financial and personal map. One way to chart your own map is to discover the roadblocks you need to avoid, the risks you need to take, and the destinations you want to reach.

A great coach named Dan Sullivan taught me to initiate talks with clients about the future by discussing their greatest *dangers*, *opportunities*, and *strengths*. We can use these same three elements to introduce you to the principles that can guide you—just as they do Emron and Aaron—in drawing up your map to financial independence. Do you identify with the following dangers? Can you grasp the opportunities ahead of you? Are you aware of these great strengths that you already possess?

What Are Some of the Dangers Twenty-Somethings Face?

Danger #1: Trying to Have Right Now What Took Your Parents Years to Acquire

When the *Wall Street Journal* asked a handful of young people about their most recent major purchases, a twenty-six-year-old, who sold advertising time for a TV network, said he had recently bought himself a giant plasma TV and two leather chairs for a total of $5,600.* They probably give him a lot of pleasure, but this fellow acknowledged that he had eight different credit cards. He admitted he opened some credit accounts for "dumb reasons," such as getting a free key chain.

Aaron has friends who spend every dollar they make buying expensive toys like the latest cell phones, video consoles, or gaming systems. Emron has friends who rent rather than own their home, but then can't wait to get the latest expensive furniture and a BMW to park in the garage. I'm sure you know peers who blow whole paychecks on a week's trip to Las Vegas or on $400 tickets to the next big concert.

Many young people love high-end games, entertainment, travel,

---

* Jennifer Saranow, *Wall Street Journal Online*, 2004, http://online.wsj.com/documents/info-actone04bio.html?starter='garcia'.

furniture, and cars—and their parents may spend the same way on these things. It's one thing to be in a position to afford these, but another to go out on a limb that could break when you max out your credit cards.

Danger #2: Saving Only 1–3 Percent of Your Income, Rather Than 10–30 Percent

The problem with allowing your love of fine things to get out of hand is that you wind up spending money you don't have yet. Then you get a credit card statement, and you can pay as much as 15 to 20 percent more on interest when you send in only the minimum amount each month.

A key to your financial future is to borrow to conserve, not to consume. Your mom and dad undoubtedly urged you to set money aside early. But perhaps they didn't specify how much of your paycheck they were talking about. Many companies that have 401(k) plans (retirement savings accounts) start by taking only 2 percent of your pretax dollars and putting them into these plans.

Do you think you can save only $20 out of every $1,000 you earn? Even 3 percent isn't very much—on a salary of $50,000 a year, that's only $1,500.

It might be that you don't want to save more than 1 to 3 percent because you are forking over $100, $200, $300, or more every month to pay down your student loans, credit card debt, and car loan. We'll discuss living within your means in chapter 4, but if you really want to get serious, be a little more frugal. Don't buy the biggest, most expensive TV, video game, or BMW yet. There's plenty of time to replace your current TV, game console, or Honda Civic.

Danger #3: Not Fully Understanding the Difference Between Preferred and Nonpreferred Debt

Most young people are advised by family, teachers, and others to get rid of any kind of debt—even debt that may be relatively inexpensive, such as a student loan. They get so preoccupied with getting this debt out of the way that they don't realize there are two kinds of debt: preferred and nonpreferred. Even some university professors advise finance students to take out a fifteen-year amortized mortgage "so you can get rid of your house mortgage early." Then, the professors say, you're in the clear—your house is paid off while you're in your thirties or forties.

We take a different view. To us, the notion that all debt is bad is just plain wrong. What we call *nonpreferred interest* is the interest you pay on a credit card or a car loan, among other things (bad debt). The interest that you pay on such things that you *consume* or that depreciate (go down in value as time goes by) is not deductible on your personal tax return. Also, you usually pay a higher rate of interest on nonpreferred debt—sometimes as high as 18 percent or more. But *preferred interest* is a tax-deductible expense and is paid on loans taken out for those things that will appreciate in value or that will help you make money (good debt). Student loans are usually regarded as "good debt" and the interest is usually deductible. When you pay interest on a mortgage or equity line on your first or second home that will likely appreciate (go up) in value, you can deduct that interest every year on Schedule A of your federal income tax return. The interest you pay on money that you borrow to buy a home should be viewed as your friend—not your foe—because you are borrowing to create wealth and *conserve* your money rather than throw it away on rent. Home mortgage money is usually the cheapest money you can borrow because the interest rates are lower and the net cost after the tax deduction results in paying effective rates as low as 4, 5, or 6 percent. *So, whenever you borrow money, you should borrow to conserve, not to consume.*

We're going to show in chapter 6 that just as a bank or credit union's greatest assets are its liabilities (because it pays interest to make more interest), you likewise can use debt to make your money flourish.

Danger #4: Not Understanding the Basics of Taxes and Paycheck Withholding

As soon as you start earning an income in the workforce, you're going to pay a lot more attention to the bite that Uncle Sam takes out of your paycheck every month. The more you make, the bigger the bite. But few young people realize that they may be paying Uncle Sam more than he requires.

Have you ever gotten a tax refund? A lot of parents will tell their kids that it's a nice present—a forced savings.

Nonsense! The government certainly is entitled to what you owe, but if you don't overpay for your food, your car, your house, or your airline tickets, why should you hand the IRS a gift of extra money month after month? In chapter 5, we'll show you how to cut down on what you pay the IRS, and how to adjust the W-4 form you fill out at work so Uncle Sam doesn't have his fingers in your pocket unnecessarily.

Danger #5: Automatically Assuming That Putting Money in IRAs and 401(k)s Is the Best Way to Save for Retirement

Chances are you've heard the terms *IRA*, for individual retirement account, and *401(k)*, which is a company-sponsored retirement plan. When you get your first serious job, the benefits department (if your company has one) makes a presentation to you about the company's 401(k) plan. Typically, the company's advisors recommend that you sock away money in that 401(k) plan, and they automatically do that for you. "Let us handle it, and we'll save money for you that's tax-deferred," they say. You say to yourself, "Hey, that sounds easy. I won't have to think about this. I'll never see the money if they take it out of my paycheck." So you sign up and you don't give it another thought.

The problem is, that may not be the best place to be putting your money, especially if your employer does not match at least 50 percent on the contributions to the plan you make. In chapter 8, we'll explain how you can easily set up a retirement plan that isn't typically offered by companies and that Uncle Sam won't take a bite out of when you're ready to collect it.

Danger #6: Assuming That "Deferring Tax" Means That You Save on Tax

The vast majority of young people don't think about taxes, much less about what the term "tax-deferred" means. It sounds good when that benefits advisor uses it in connection with the pitch on the 401(k) plan.

It sounds even better when the company will "match," or kick in, an additional amount—such as 50 percent of your contribution. That's "free money," right? Not quite. Tax-deferred does not mean tax-free. Ultimately, your employer's contributions probably will end up just covering your tax for you. That is, most likely all of the growth on the matching amount will end up belonging to the Internal Revenue Service.

That's right: The federal government effectively has a tax lien on you that it will collect years from now. We'll show you that when you put away "pretax" dollars in a 401(k), you're just postponing the inevitable, because Uncle Sam fully intends to collect that money later.

If you were a farmer, would you rather save tax on the purchase of your seed during spring and pay tax on the sale of your harvest in the fall? Or would you rather pay tax on the seed and sell your harvest without any tax on the gain? We'll return to this question in chapter 5.

Danger #7: Assuming That the Government or Your Employer Will Provide a Comfortable Retirement

A lot of young people are ignorant about Social Security. They don't realize that a chunk of each paycheck goes into the antiquated federal Social Security system. The problem is that the money young people hand over to Social Security is for the security of their parents' generation, not their own. Because the Social Security system is so stretched, that government piggy bank might be empty by the time the younger generation is ready to tap into it.

You probably also have seen—even firsthand through the experience of your parents or friends—that when companies get into trouble, they take away employer benefits that they had promised their employees. Those are indeed concerns. More and more of you will have to provide for your own retirement. In chapter 8, we will show you how you can develop your own plan so you don't have to rely on others.

But what if you're one of those who thinks, "I've spent $30,000 a year to go to college; the world owes me a living"? Get real! This is a new era. Your parents might have thought that retirement pension plans with large companies like Chrysler, General Motors, and Ford would be around forever. But many large companies have been forced to change, reduce, or eliminate retirement benefits. What might have been true during the industrial revolution and in the twentieth century might be totally different for the twenty-first.

Danger #8: Buying and Selling Investments at the Wrong Time, Rather Than Buying and Holding

This is the most common investing mistake made by Americans young and old. People put money they plan to hold for the long term into short-term investments, such as certificates of deposit, money market funds, or other investments that earn a very small interest rate—even though they don't plan to touch it for ten, twenty, or more years. Then they latch on to news of a hot stock or mutual fund. Suddenly they are taking some of that "long-term" money to buy a risky investment hoping for a short-term gain—a thousand shares of that hot stock. What if it grows cold? They get impatient when the stock goes down and sell it at a loss. Young people can be especially impatient about letting money grow over time.

However, the real secret of wealth accumulation is to put money aside, keep it aside, and put it to work for you. Interest rates or rates of return are not as important as systematic savings. As we'll show later on, it's fine to have a "put and take" account (a checking account with a debit card for those trips to the ATM or drive-up window) for necessary month-to-month expenses. But we'll show you how to create a "put and keep" account for the long term—how to buy the right investments built for the long haul, and how to hold them, rather than raiding your long-term accounts when you get an urge to spend.

Danger #9: Viewing the World with a "Scarcity" Mentality

You've undoubtedly heard people say that this is a "dog-eat-dog" world. Too many Americans in every age category feel, "I've got to get ahead because there's not enough to go around." Whether it comes from competing in sports or from professors who graded everyone on a bell-shaped curve, a lot of young people develop the mentality of scarcity. Perhaps you felt in school that only a certain number of students in each class could be awarded an A.

The idea that "others must fail for me to succeed" is deeply ingrained in some Americans. Emron recalls, "That was the feeling in classes of all kinds, from finance to chemistry. But especially if they were honors classes, everybody wanted to excel. They felt it came down to the idea that someone had to lose in order for you to win."

Some feel that this sense of edging others out is the biggest cause of cheating in the educational system. It is also one reason why so many young athletes feel they have to take steroids. The thinking is, "Everyone else is doing it, so if I want to be as good as the steroid cheaters, I'll have to take steroids too."

We want to show you that if you look at life as a feast of abundance, you see opportunities instead of threats, gains rather than losses—in finance and in life.

Danger #10: Focusing on the Least Important Categories on the Family Balance Sheet: Money, Rather Than Relationships

The most important thing to many young people today is becoming wealthy, according to polls. "But those polls only mention financial wealth, rather than two other areas—human assets and intellectual assets," says Aaron. We believe that you need to start making alliances and learning work skills from others. Whether it's learning from their work ethic, values, compassion, or sense of leadership, you can look to parents, extended family, community leaders, and work colleagues to accumulate important social, personal, and intellectual assets.

How can you build healthy relationships at work? The world loves usefulness, and you should be useful to those you work with, including your bosses. Simply punching a time clock to get a paycheck doesn't do much for work relationships. We'll talk more in chapter 10 about healthy work relationships and developing your personal, social, and intellectual assets.

What Are Your Greatest Opportunities?

Opportunity #1: Realizing You've Got Plenty of Time to Learn, Even Make Mistakes, Then Recover

When you are in your early twenties, you are likely to be single and have no children yet.* That gives you an awesome opportunity to make financial moves without the concern of having to support anyone but yourself. It's an ideal time to buy a rental property, for example. We'll talk about that in chapter 7.

In addition to pursuing formal education, you can explore other learning experiences beyond the classroom—ones that add to your real-life knowledge. Both Emron and Aaron, for example, went on voluntary two-year church missions right out of high school, which they helped pay for out of their own pockets.

Emron spent two years in Japan and learned to speak Japanese. Aaron spent his missionary years among Latino communities in

---

* The estimated median age of marriage in the United States is twenty-seven for men and twenty-five for women. From http://www.census.gov/population/socdemo/hh-fam/ms2.pdf.

and near New York City. These were years that taught them volumes about life, service, and communicating with people from cultures different from their own. They had not yet completed college, but their missions gave them an alternative kind of higher education. Emron puts it this way: "During those two years, I gained probably *ten years in knowledge and experience*, and I know that has helped me."

Whether it's volunteering for a religious mission, enrolling in a study abroad program, helping out on a charitable expedition, spending a year working overseas, serving your country, or even getting involved in community programs close to home, you can find "real-life" ways to augment your knowledge and skills.

Opportunity #2: Being Flexible in Your Career and Life Choices

Baby Boomer parents may have spent thirty years in the same job. But according to recent studies, those of you now in your twenties might switch careers or occupations seven different times between the time you graduate from college and the time you retire.

By being flexible in your career and life choices, you are opening yourself up to new opportunities to learn and bring value to the world. Just as it's not unusual for college students to switch their majors from pre-med to English to finance during their undergraduate years, you may find as you start your career that there are other passions and interests that lead you to make a change in your professional path. Be open to change; weigh your options; and be ready for a touch of serendipity in your life.

Perhaps one of the best ways to do this is to continually enlarge your circle—get to know a variety of people with different areas of expertise. Learn from their knowledge; see different points of view; add to your own abilities. You can also read books or enroll in seminars with executive coaches. Aaron makes a habit of meeting informally with real estate agents to keep abreast of the local market. A friend who is a computer artist keeps up on his field through blogs and discussion groups on the Web.

Opportunity #3: Finding Prudent Ways to Create Multiple Streams of Income and Moneymaking Opportunities

Shortly, we will go into more detail on the three sources of income: people at work, money at work, and charity. For now, let's just talk about the first. Aaron's friend the computer artist supplements his primary income by freelancing at home. My son-in-law Scott buys and sells things on eBay, and he's not alone. We've heard that the federal Bureau of Labor Statistics is considering adjusting its employment data because so many Americans moonlight, with some making $50,000 to $100,000 in these second jobs.

You may be among those who are earning money through additional jobs. If you are, it's often hard work, and we commend you. But the good news is there are other ways to generate multiple streams of income. Soon, we'll discuss how owning rental property can create positive cash flow for you.

Opportunity #4: Looking at the World's Problems and Coming Up with Solutions That Society Will Pay You For

Negative thinkers might focus on what's wrong with today's world, but positive "possibility thinkers" look for solutions. Sometimes these solutions are commodities or services that people are willing to pay for, which could mean additional income for you.

For example, when the world was apprehensive that the Y2K glitch might disrupt modern life, a few smart young entrepreneurs packaged a "72–hour kit" and built it into a business. It's a backpack that contains all the items a household might need in an emergency, including three days' worth of food, water purification tablets, space blankets, a flashlight, batteries, and so on. The kits are still selling today, long after the Y2K scare, and one manufacturer has added "Office Disaster Kits" and "Bird Flu Kits" to its line.

Opportunity #5: The Chance to Be in Motion and Add Value, for Which the World Will Compensate You

Rather than being an employee who just puts in the required hours, you can start becoming a problem solver and offer improvement ideas to your employer that demonstrate how much you can contribute. Being a problem solver means being alert and willing to implement new ideas.

Emron did this for our financial services company. He saw that we needed specific software to support our financial planning system, something that could tally a client's financial holdings and then customize solutions and products needed to optimize wealth. In his spare time, he wrote out mathematical formulas and worked with a programmer who translated the numbers into computer code. After putting in hundreds of hours, they introduced the software. It has since been refined, and we market the software to asset and liability advisors, who have found it valuable for their clients. It began as a need, then a solution, and now it grosses hundreds of thousands of dollars.

Opportunity #6: The Chance to Buy Your First House

Now is the time to look seriously at buying your first house. It is definitely a big step, but one of the most important when it comes to the "millionaire mindset" that we will discuss in chapter 3. There are many advantages that come with buying real estate. You may be thinking, "There is no way I am ready to buy a house." In upcoming chapters we will show that you might be closer than you think. We will also disclose unique ways on how you can purchase your first home sooner rather than later using very little or none of your own money for the down payment.

With home ownership comes a new attitude of responsibility and accountability. Once you take this step you will learn so much more about finance, budgeting, and money. There is a sense of financial maturity that comes with buying that first home. Keep reading and we will show you how to seize this incredible opportunity to catapult you financially in numerous ways.

What Are the Greatest Strengths You Possess?

Perhaps the greatest strengths that reside in young adults are an optimistic outlook, a vibrant attitude, and a zest for living. You are not jaded or cynical about what you can accomplish, and hopefully you have not suffered too many personal or financial knocks that make older people tentative. But you possess many more strengths.

Strength #1: Researching and Finding Information Quickly

A special skill that so many members of your age group have is your familiarity with technology. Because you have grown up with Web-based communication, you are generally much faster and more competent at researching information and connecting with others online, whether it's on your laptop, cell phone, or PDA.

You probably already have jumped on the Web to do background checks on jobs you are offered, not to mention surveying Facebook, MySpace, and YouTube for details on people and events.

You can use these skills to research investments, real estate, and every other aspect of personal finance. You can maximize your understanding of technology to learn more, earn more, and experience more.

Strength #2: Communicating More Quickly, Easily, and Globally

While the ease of communicating quickly and globally is available to everyone, young adults are truly in stride with the warp speed of today's communications. Aaron tells people that all his mother does with the telephone is talk, but just a few years ago that was all you could do with a phone. Today, young people can crank out text messages in seconds—many of them without even looking down at their PDAs or cell phones.

When I was in Japan and Korea in 2005, I saw young people on the subway hunched over their cell phones, and I thought they were playing games. But they were communicating with others. When we went on a family vacation to Hawaii, my daughter Ashley sent photos of our family scuba diving to friends on the mainland just minutes after it happened.

Your ease with global communications puts you at an advantage to connect with others around the world, pushing your aspirations, ideas, and talents literally much farther than any previous generation could.

Strength #3: Having Greater Mobility Than Previous Generations

In my hometown, some people I grew up with never got out of the state of Utah before they reached their thirties and forties. Today, young Americans don't view moving frequently as a barrier. When you combine today's mobility with your technology skills and ability to communicate globally, you can harness twenty-first-century tools for significant personal, intellectual, and occupational accomplishments.

Emron and Aaron know peers who have moved to California for jobs they discovered on national online employment Web sites. Emron's brother-in-law travels constantly for his job. Both Emron and Aaron have clients across the United States with whom they can routinely conduct business via Web conferencing and e-mail. When face time becomes important, it's so much easier now than it was for me twenty years ago to hop on a plane and visit someone in person.

Mobility also allows you to seek business opportunities and monitor contacts, products, or real estate far more easily than ever before. Conversely, new products make it easier to be mobile. Young adults who are pretty sure they are not going to live in a certain area for more than a few years can take advantage of creative new mortgage offerings, which we will discuss in chapters 6 and 7. When they are ready to move, they can easily cruise through houses for sale in far-flung locations on the Internet before ever physically seeing them.

Strength #4: The Ability to Take Risks

Young adults, especially when they are still single, can take more risks than older people because their lives are often less tied down.

Whether it's the unpredictability of working on commission, experiencing ups and downs in the market, or testing new financial planning strategies, the impact of financial risks tends to be less when a person is just starting out. For example, if a single twenty-five-year-old were to face a few slow months with less commission, she could eat mac and cheese, shop at the discount store, and make ends meet until things pick up. Her circumstances would be much more difficult if she were a thirty-five-year-old wife and mother of three with a larger mortgage, two car payments, and myriad family expenses.

While young, take advantage of your flexibility and relatively fewer responsibilities to explore opportunities and learn from any mistakes.

Strength #5: Ingenuity in Creating Unique Products

Brett, a twenty-eight-year-old friend of Aaron's, is putting everything on the line to be an entrepreneur. He got his start-up money by winning thousands of dollars in a contest his university held for the best entrepreneurial ideas. He identified the need for a unique kind of recreational shoe, confirmed it by talking to experts at the Outdoor Retailer industry show, found a designer, and then flew to China to meet manufacturers. Brett is an example of how you can take risks, utilize the global economy, and make the latest communications and computer technologies work for you.

Here's another example. About a decade ago, eighteen-year-old Utahn Shawn Nelson decided to reinvent the 1970s idea of the beanbag chair. He came up with an oversized version, caught the attention of a very large retailer, got an advance deposit on the retailer's order to start production, found a manufacturer in China to make his retro bag (which he called the LoveSac), and ultimately won the $1 million first prize on the Fox network's reality TV show *Rebel Billionaire*. LoveSac sells its products on the Internet and also has a chain of retail outlets across the United States.

Strength #6: Resilience—the Ability to Bounce Back and Start Over

In 1978, when I was twenty-six years old and married just four years, Sharee and I built our third home—a beautiful 6,400–square-foot, six-bedroom house located on a canyon rim. We did not make the mistake of tying up any of our own money in the house while building it. Shortly after we moved in, the house appraised for $300,000 and we only owed $150,000 on the mortgage. Four years later, three things happened to us that we never dreamed would happen simultaneously, and we found ourselves without an income for about nine months.

In desperation, we sold other assets to keep our mortgage payments current, but we were soon forced to put the house up for sale. Because it was a soft real estate market (more homes for sale than interested buyers), we were also forced to eventually lower the sales price of the house to under $200,000. It didn't help. We ended up losing the house in foreclosure after we got three months behind on our mortgage payments. We learned a valuable lesson from that experience that has helped us and hundreds of our clients: It's better to have access to your home equity and not need it than to need it and not be able to get it.

When I lost my house in foreclosure in 1982, I was thirty years old. My mother was distraught. At that age I thought, "It's no big deal, Mom. I can buy another house with nothing down." And I did. I may still be more of a risk-taker than some, but when you are young, you are resilient—you can absorb a setback and then bounce back faster; you have more time ahead of you. You are able to learn from your mistakes.

It's the same with any entrepreneurial project that might fail. Resilience is the ability to attack and adjust; you attack a project or idea, and then because you're in motion adding value, you can adjust your product or marketing scheme. If necessary, you can step back, regroup, and start over. It's like football—if you get sacked, or your team is down by ten points in the second quarter, you can punt and still have plenty of time for a comeback victory.

Strength #7: Learning from History and Avoiding the Mistakes of the Past

Here is Emron's perspective: "As young people we have a bank of knowledge from our parents and extended family—many of them from the Baby Boom generation. We can ask what has worked for them and what hasn't worked. If we find someone we want to emulate, our task is find out from them what they would do if they had the chance to do it all over again."

Aaron adds, "You can learn a great deal from older people who are in the same field as you are. If you're going to be a physician, talk to a physician ten years ahead of you. Ask him or her, 'When it comes to finances, what would you have done differently?'"

When it comes to building your future, you have the opportunity at this point in your young adult years to avoid the dangers, seize the opportunities, and maximize your strengths. You can take ownership of your finances and create your own vision to achieve financial independence in your thirties. In the next chapters, we'll explain how.

REMEMBER THIS

- Understand and avoid the top ten dangers you face in securing your future, whether it is choosing the wrong retirement plan, not saving enough money, or misunderstanding the nature of taxes.
- Understand that your youth, flexibility, and ability to earn money and put it to work are among your greatest opportunities.
- Recognize that your strengths include your ability to take risks, to be mobile, to bounce back from mistakes, and to profit from technology and global communications.
- Understand that age is not a detriment and lack of resources is not a hindrance to wealth accumulation. Knowledge and time will overcome the lack of money and resources.
- Once you have identified your greatest dangers, opportunities, and strengths, you can map your brighter future with much greater clarity, balance, focus, and confidence to effectively avoid those dangers, seize your greatest opportunities, and harness your best strengths.
- By being responsible and accountable, you can take ownership of your future and enjoy choice and control with regard to time, money, relationships, and your purpose for working and living as you please.

LEARNING LINKS

- To help you identify and personalize your own dangers, opportunities, and strengths through a self-conducted exercise, please visit www.MissedFortune.com/Millionaire-By-Thirty and click on the learning portal for chapter 2.

CHAPTER 3

The Millionaire Mindset

Harness the Power of Three to Simplify Your Finances

AT THIS POINT, PERHAPS YOU feel a little overwhelmed, and you wonder whether financial planning is just too complex for you.

Let's play a game of sticks. It will show you how easy it can be to get going, to put yourself and your finances in motion.

Take a blank piece of paper and draw twenty-one lines on it, like sticks. You play against us. We alternate in crossing off either one or two sticks. The winner is the side that captures the final stick(s).

You go first. Let's assume you take one stick. At this moment, right at the beginning, we can tell you that we will beat you. How? Because we're not really talking about all twenty-one sticks, we're talking about one plus two, which equals three sticks. We take two sticks, and the page is reduced to eighteen. As long as the remainder is divisible by three, it doesn't matter whether you cross out one or two; we simply take the opposite of what you take. Go ahead: it's your turn. You take two. We take one. That leaves fifteen. You take one. We take two, and so on.

We win this game of twenty-one sticks every time if we are second to choose. You can win a game of *twenty* sticks every time if you *start* the game and take two sticks first and then do the opposite of your opponent every round thereafter. Once you reduce the game to its most simple form (a game of three sticks), it doesn't matter whether you are playing a game starting with twenty sticks, thirty sticks, sixty sticks, or any other number. You can win this game the majority of the time if you are aware that it is really only a game of three sticks played a multiple of times.

In the same way, too many people view investment strategies as having ten or twenty elements. College students are used to thinking in terms of studying something for a whole semester before being comfortable putting what they learn into practice. But the "millionaire mindset" aims to keep things simple, so you can act right now.

We will help you win the game of finances by narrowing many topics to groups of three. For the rest of this book, we'll focus on issues such as the three types of income, the three things you can do with money, and so forth.

After a public seminar that I gave, a recent college graduate came up to me and said, "In these three hours, I've learned more from you than I did in all my years at college—and I majored in finance! We just studied all the time. You've shown me how to apply all that knowledge."

You don't have to be a college graduate to put these concepts into practice right now. We'll make things as simple as possible so you will have what you need to accumulate wealth and be on the way to becoming a millionaire by your thirties.

Three Phases of Financial Maturity

Are you a *Striver,* an *Arriver,* or a *Thriver* in your approach to money? Lee Brower, the founder of Empowered Wealth LC, of which I am a national advisory board member, was the first to name these stages of financial maturity. This is our simple adaptation of his categories.

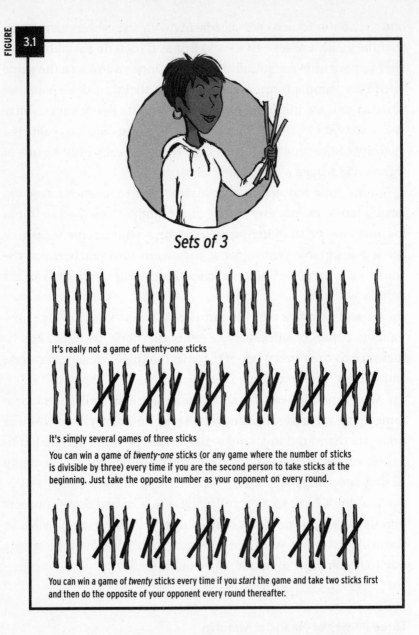

FIGURE 3.1

Sets of 3

It's really not a game of twenty-one sticks

It's simply several games of three sticks

You can win a game of *twenty-one* sticks (or any game where the number of sticks is divisible by three) every time if you are the second person to take sticks at the beginning. Just take the opposite number as your opponent on every round.

You can win a game of *twenty* sticks every time if you *start* the game and take two sticks first and then do the opposite of your opponent every round thereafter.

Strivers are the millions of people who may want to manage their money better but who don't understand the dynamics of money yet. They are often what I refer to as financial jellyfish. Jellyfish are invertebrates—they have no skeletal structure. They also do not have a specialized central nervous, digestive, respiratory, or circulatory system. They are slow swimmers—having limited control over movement—and usually free-float or drift as they are tossed to and fro by the ocean currents. At some of the reefs where our family scuba dives, when the waves get rough, the unstable jellyfish sometimes get torn to pieces, and swimmers can be stung by coming into contact with a torn-off tentacle.

Likewise, many Strivers are like the unstable jellyfish. They drift through life aimlessly, with no structure, and they often "fall apart" during rough times. They live only in the present. They only want to know how to make money and then spend it. These are the people who keep all their "savings" in a no-interest checking account and hit the nearest ATM every time they need cash, paying a fee every time. They often spend the money they are going to earn three months down the road by misusing credit cards. They borrow to consume, not to conserve.

Arrivers were once Strivers, but by applying some discipline and knowledge about managing their money, they have set out on the path to a true wealth transformation. They have learned about principles such as the three marvels of wealth accumulation, which we'll introduce shortly.

Thrivers are one rung above Arrivers on the ladder. They have learned how to repeat the process of accumulating wealth over and over again. They are the people like Emron and Aaron who by the age of thirty have acquired a primary home and a second home.

Do you want to be a Striver or Arriver for the next thirty or forty years, and just get by? Wouldn't you rather be a financially independent Thriver? Consider this as your step-by-step guidebook to becoming a Thriver. We will teach you to understand how to harness lazy, idle cash that you did not know existed, how to apply the three marvels to make it grow, and how to repeat the process over and over.

If you are concerned about how to absorb these concepts, remember that the teaching method of threes will help you retain the information.

FIGURE 3.2

"Striver - No Ownership"

"Arriver - Home Ownership"

"Thriver - Multiple Ownership"

Three Sources of Income

There are three principal sources of income:

1) People at work
2) Money at work
3) Charity

You may think you can be financially stable by working for the rest of your life, but with life's uncertainties (illnesses, layoffs, market crashes, etc.), that may not be true. However, you can always put your money to work. Having your money at work means it never needs a day off; it works 24/7, as the magic of compound interest accumulates. You can be out with your boat, on your skis, or enjoying a trip to Cancún, and it doesn't matter—your money can keep working even while you're playing. The essence of this book is to show you that by your thirties, you can have your money earning more than *you* do by working.

As we mentioned briefly earlier, it's far more predictable and secure to have your money earning income for you than for you to earn it yourself. Life is unpredictable—accidents, illness, or family emergencies occur that can disrupt the best-laid plans. You won't get a lot of advance warning if there is a serious economic recession that puts you out of work, or if your employer falls on hard times and is forced to downsize. And then there are those "unthinkable" events, such as Hurricane Katrina, a tornado, or an earthquake, that might interrupt your ability to earn a living.

It is often said that young people think they are immortal. The reality is, of course, you're not. In fact, you may not have the capacity to work for as many years as you think. Look around and you'll see living, breathing wake-up calls among your parents' generation.

When adults hit age fifty or sixty, large numbers of them discover that for one reason or another, their usefulness declines, and they find it harder to land a new job when deprived of their previous one. Health issues make some of them less mobile or less willing to endure long hours, whether it is in an office, doing construction, or driving an eighteen-wheeler across the country.

Do you really want to wait until you are in your fifties to have your money working for you? Or would you rather have the security of knowing that by your thirties, if you wanted to go back to school to switch professions, or if you were laid off, or if the world had a disaster like 9/11, your money would be earning enough to keep the wolves away from the door?

Three Things to Do with Money

There are three things you can do with money:

- Spend it
- Lend it
- Own with it

If you are like most of your peers, you probably know a lot about the joy of spending—whether it is on designer-label clothes, cars, sports gear, travel, dining out, movies, concerts, or the latest technology item. In chapter 4, we'll go into detail on how to keep your spending under control.

How much do you know about lending and owning? If asked, most people would say they would rather have their money in an ownership position than in a lended position. Well, it's good to own something—especially real estate. We'll talk a lot about that in upcoming chapters. We will go into detail about the three types of real estate you should own by the time you are thirty:

- A personal residence
- A second home/vacation rental
- A rental income property

If you put your money in a bank, a credit union, a bond, a mutual fund, or an insurance contract, you are lending it. You think you are "saving" or "investing." But in fact you are lending the institution your money by choice. Banks and credit unions make millions by using *other people's money* (OPM). They pay you one rate (interest) for your money, and then lend it to others at a higher rate. They are using OPM—yours—to earn even more money. That's why, as we said before, a bank's greatest assets are its liabilities. In chapter 6, we teach you how you can use OPM, just like banks do, to start building your fortune, even if you do not yet have a credit history.

Three Marvels of Wealth Accumulation

These are the three keys to supercharging your assets. They are not really magic, but they are as crucial to wealth as the concepts of lift, thrust, and drag are to aerodynamics. They are:

- The magic of compound interest (lift)
- The magic of tax-favored accumulation (thrust)
- The magic of safe, positive leverage using OPM (drag)

The hardest concept for people of all ages to understand is "drag." Once, when I discussed these at a seminar, a pilot came up to me afterward. "I've flown for years now, but I still don't understand, why do I need drag?" he asked. Bear with us and you'll understand why just as lift, thrust, and drag are essential to flight, the same principles can make your money take wing.

Imagine you've just taken up kiteboarding. To propel yourself on your board across the water, you need four forces: weight, lift, thrust, and drag. In finance, we think of weight, which is really the pull of gravity, as similar to taxes and inflation. Weight is always involved in aerodynamics, as taxes and inflation are in finance.

But for your kite to get airborne, you need *lift*—the force of air flowing over and under that piece of fabric. We compare lift to the power of compound interest.

To propel yourself forward, you need *thrust*—harnessing the wind's power against the kite, giving you momentum to plane across the water. We compare thrust to the power of tax-favored accumulation, a financial thrust that we explain in chapter 8.

Finally, to keep yourself gliding across the water, you must

FIGURE **3.3**

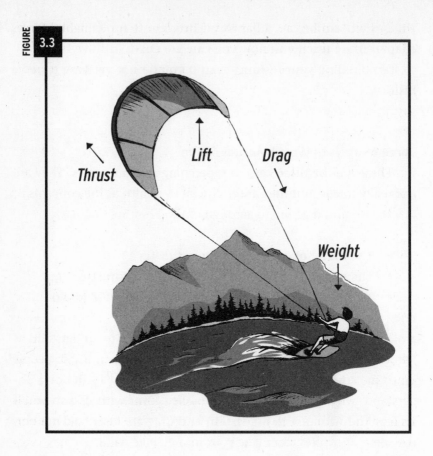

Thrust

Lift

Drag

Weight

create resistance against the kite. That's *drag*. When you feel that resistance, your board suddenly will accelerate. We compare drag to the power of safe, positive leverage—using other people's money from a bank or mortgage. To understand the importance of drag, imagine letting go of the rope. What happens? Your forward motion stops and you begin to sink.

When the pilot at the seminar started imagining these elements working together, it was as if a lightbulb had been turned on—he brightened, grinned, and said, "Now I get it." These aerodynamic principles are the same, whether you are kiteboarding or you're at the controls of a gigantic five-hundred-passenger jetliner taking off the ground. And in a similar way, Thrivers use fundamental forces to make their money climb to new heights.

Now, despite the explanation, you may be wondering why we use the word "drag," especially when that sounds negative. Because just as drag makes your kite soar, your savings start escalating into wealth when you borrow money for leverage and pay interest on it. What's more, *you reduce the drag by streamlining the cost of borrowing if the interest is tax-deductible.* In upcoming chapters, we will go into these key forces in more detail.

Three Attitudes Toward Interest

Here's another concept that many people misunderstand. You may have been cautioned about interest by professors or your parents, who say that there are only two kinds of people: those who *pay* interest, and those who *earn* interest.

We're introducing the third and most successful kind: people who pay interest to earn *more* interest.

We've emphasized that a bank or credit union's greatest asset is its liabilities—that is, its debts. If institutions like banks did not borrow other people's money, they would wither and die. They must borrow, so they accept deposits, which are actually "loans" from people like you, and they pay you one rate of interest. Then they turn around and lend the same money to people and companies—but they charge them a higher interest rate, which adds up and makes millions of dollars in profits.

The Super Thrivers of the world do exactly the same thing. As we'll show a bit later, anyone who gets a mortgage is borrowing money. The Super Thrivers are happy to save their own money and pay a small amount of interest when they finance a home purchase, because they can put their money to work to earn a much greater return over time. What's more, Uncle Sam becomes their partner, because they are permitted to use mortgage interest as a tax deduction.

Anyone in a hurry to pay off a student loan should pause before sending off extra payments on it. Why? *Because your savings or discretionary dollars are way too valuable to use on student loans, which may carry a relatively low interest rate.* (As of this writing, the rate on most student loans taken out before June 2006 was 7.14 percent.)* You can continue to make minimum payments on a student loan while putting your dollars into investments that earn you a higher rate.

A word of caution, however. We are *not* suggesting that you run up debt on a *credit card* in order to get money for speculative investments. Credit card interest rates are typically a lot higher than student loan interest rates. Too many young adults borrow against their credit card limit to chase the latest hot stock. The next thing you know, the stock loses value, leaving those speculators with oodles of money owed on an expensive credit card. It's a great way to ruin your credit standing. Always be conservative, not aggressive, when it comes to borrowing.

We'll have a lot more to say in upcoming chapters about the smartest, most sensible ways to pay interest in order to earn more interest.

Three Lodging Places for Money

The money that you set aside and accumulate for long-range goals should be kept in a place where it can reside safely. There are three categories where people park their money for investment purposes, based on their risk tolerance:

- Low-risk, stable investments (houses of bricks)
- Moderate-risk investments (houses of sticks)
- Higher-risk investments (houses of straw)

The first category contains those generally regarded as the safest and most conservative investments. These include money market

---

* http://ifap.ed.gov/dlbulletins/attachments/DLB0605Attach.pdf.

accounts, certificates of deposit (CDs), bonds, annuities, and insurance contracts. The second category includes real estate—both residential and commercial. Most real estate investments pose moderate risk. The third category includes stocks and growth mutual funds. This category is generally viewed as having the greatest risk.

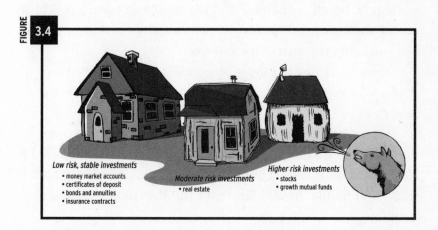

FIGURE 3.4

Low risk, stable investments
- money market accounts
- certificates of deposit
- bonds and annuities
- insurance contracts

Moderate risk investments
- real estate

Higher risk investments
- stocks
- growth mutual funds

People tend to move their money from one category to another when they lose patience or get nervous about how that category is performing. For example, in the early 1980s people tended to keep money predominantly in bonds, money markets, CDs, annuities, and life insurance contracts. Many investors also parked their money in real estate. Why? Because they didn't trust the stock market.

Then in the 1990s, as the stock market gained steam in its largest run-up in history, a lot of money was transferred to the stock market from more conservative investments. From 1980 until 2000, gains in stocks were about 500 percent. That may sound like a significant return, but it really represents only an 8.38 percent annual increase. In other words, a $10,000 investment earning 8.38 percent interest compounded annually will grow 500 percent to $50,000 in twenty years.

In early spring of 2000, the Dow Jones Industrial Average hit 11,900, and net inflows into the market totaled $50 billion—people buying high. Unfortunately, the stock market turned sour after that. The worst three years in stock market history (by percentage loss and by dollar loss) occurred during a period from the spring of 2000 into 2003. By the summer of 2002, the Dow bottomed out at 7,500, and there was a net outflow of $50 billion—people selling low.

At that point a lot of people were transferring their money to real estate, bonds, annuities, and life insurance contracts. This is one of the major reasons for the real estate boom during the first five years after the turn of the century.

Money must find a lodging place, and when it leaves one of the three repositories described above, it migrates over to one or both of the other two.

It takes people time to regain faith in the stock market once they have taken a beating. As the market started to shoot upward in 2007, seasoned investors once again began moving money back to stocks and mutual funds.* But that's still the riskiest lodging place for money.

Our financial strategies are designed so you can take advantage of all three lodging places, or categories. Later on in this book, we'll discuss how to choose the most prudent investments, which meet the LSRR—pronounced "LASER"—test of maintaining *liquidity*, *safety of principal*, and *rate of return* on serious cash. For now, all you need is a basic understanding of what these three terms mean.

- *Liquidity* means you can get your money back when you want it. Think about the sign that you often see at a furniture or car dealership: "Liquidation Sale." It means the store is selling its inventory at a discount to turn it into cash quickly.
- *Safety* means that the principal cash you have invested is guaranteed or insured. No matter whether a market goes up or down, you are protected.

---

* http://blogs.wsj.com/marketbeat/2007/04/27/five-reasons-why-the-rally-continues/.

- Finally, you want the greatest *rate of return* with the least amount of risk on your investments. There are always trade-offs, but later on we'll guide you to the most prudent investments that pass the "LASER" test.

In chapter 9, we will show you how to use leverage safely to achieve rates of return that are *linked* to a stock index, while your money is actually not at risk *in* the stock market. Your cash can be invested safely in conservative investment vehicles that will compound in a tax-advantaged environment where it is accessible and safe employing the three marvels. You'll learn how you can have the best of both worlds: taking advantage of the upswings in the stock market or real estate market, without having your principal at risk in the market.

The point is that we prefer to keep what we call "serious cash"— money for the long haul—in safe places. We want to make sure we get maximum results with minimal risk. Later on, we'll show you that if the big bad wolf (hurricanes, floods, tornadoes, fires, terrorist attacks, market crashes, etc.) threatens to blow down the structures that hold stocks (houses made of straw) and real estate holdings (houses made of sticks), you won't lose—because your money resides in a house of bricks.

We'll also talk later about what moves you can make when "houses of straw" or "houses of sticks" stand up for periods of calm weather and appreciate in value. We'll show you how to participate in that growth without actually parking your money there. If they blow over, you'll stay protected. In other words, we'll show you how to invest wisely so you sleep better at night, regardless of economic or market swings.

Three Types of Taxable Income

It's important to understand how the federal government and the Internal Revenue Service collect taxes from you. Bear with us now, because this is not the most exciting concept in this book. In order to get to the sweet juicy center of an orange, it's necessary to dig through the bitter peel that surrounds the fruit. In the same way, some financial topics are perhaps not bitter, but rather dry, like this one. But spend a little time reading these few paragraphs, and later on you'll enjoy the sweet reward that comes from understanding how the IRS taxes certain investments but doesn't tax others.

For more than twenty years (since the Tax Reform Act of 1986) there have been only three types of income that are taxed by the federal government:

- Earned income
- Passive income
- Portfolio income

You probably already have *earned income*—that's the money you make for providing goods or services. This is the money you earn from your job.

If your money is working for you, it is earning either passive or portfolio income. *Portfolio income* is the money usually realized through interest and dividends paid on savings and investments, stocks, and so forth.

Passive income is money that typically is realized through rental income from real estate property or leases. If you've rented an apartment, town home, condo, or house, the money you pay as rent to your landlord is passive income for the landlord. He or she doesn't have to pay Social Security or Medicare on it. Landlords with passive income also get to take deductions on their taxes based upon mortgage payments or the expenses they incur for owning that apartment that they rented to you. In a short while, you'll see how you can start *receiving* rental income, instead of paying rent.

Later on, we'll go into more detail on some absolutely legal tax breaks that can save you thousands of dollars. We will also introduce you to the three best investments for portfolio income that meet the "LASER" test. And we'll introduce the one investment among them that triggers absolutely *no income tax* at all if you follow the advice we'll offer later in this book.

Three Phases in Saving Tax-Advantaged Money for the Future

You are years away from "retirement" as your parents and grandparents defined it. The old notion of retirement meant leaving a job after twenty, thirty, or thirty-five years, getting a gold watch, and collecting a pension. But far fewer young adults follow this traditional career path. You may work for one company for only a few years before switching to a new one or going out on your own. Meanwhile, old-fashioned pensions are almost as extinct as dinosaurs.

Most companies suggest that employees take part in a different kind of retirement plan, usually referred to as a 401(k). You have likely heard about 401(k) plans and individual retirement accounts (IRAs). We will talk in detail about those later on.

For now, the key concepts we would like you to understand are that there are three phases of saving in these plans—the contribution phase, the accumulation phase, and the distribution phase. When you develop a systematic plan for the future, you have three alternatives:

- A plan that gives you tax breaks on the contribution and accumulation phases
- A plan that gives you tax breaks on the accumulation and distribution phases
- A strategy that can give you tax breaks on all three phases—contribution, accumulation, and distribution.

Earlier, we posed this question: If you were a farmer, and you had a choice, which would you rather do—save taxes on the seed you bought in the spring and then pay tax on the sale of your harvest in the fall, or pay tax on the seed now and sell your harvest without any tax on the gain? Now here's a third alternative: How much more powerful is it to get tax breaks on *both* the seed and the harvest?

In upcoming chapters, we will explain how you can set up a savings plan for the future that puts your money in position to grow in a tax-favored environment during the contribution and accumulation phases (the seed), as well as the distribution phase (harvest). It is a strategy that is smarter than any plan created by the government or by your employer. And we have a hunch that even your CPA does not know about it.

This is what we mean by the "millionaire mindset." We are about to help you design a financial strategy that lets you accumulate enough money by your mid-thirties so that your money is earning as much as you do—or more—*for the rest of your life*. What counts is not what you begin with, but what you end up with.

When you reach that point in your thirties, you can decide if you want to continue to work. But that does not mean "retirement" in the old-fashioned sense. One definition of retirement is to be "put out of use." We want to dispel that idea. We put machinery out of use; we don't retire human ingenuity.

We want you to have security not in a job, but in yourself as an individual. We want you to become financially independent so you can live the life you have always dreamed about and do whatever you choose to do, by your mid-thirties.

The millionaire mindset means starting with a vision and having clear goals. So right now, start to harness your own "power of three." In the space below, jot down answers to these questions that can help guide you on your route to financial independence:

- What are my three most serious financial dangers?

  _____

  _____

  _____

- What are my three major barriers to financial health?

  _____

  _____

  _____

- What are my three greatest abilities?

  _____

  _____

  _____

Now jot down these visions for your future:

- Three opportunities to use these abilities to generate income:

  _____

  _____

  _____

- Three places I most want to visit or experiences to enjoy:

  _____

  _____

  _____

- Three ways I can give back to society:

  _____

  _____

  _____

REMEMBER THIS

- The millionaire mindset begins by harnessing the power of threes to simplify your finances.
- Paying preferred interest will help you soar financially and help you become your own banker by borrowing money at a lower rate and investing it at a slightly higher rate.
- Money at work is a more predictable and secure source of income, and it never takes a vacation—it works 24/7.
- You can have your serious cash tucked safely in a "house of bricks" and still participate indirectly when "houses of straw and sticks" (the stock or real estate markets) are doing well, but not lose when those markets are not doing well.
- Choose to be a Thriver—a person who understands strategies to accumulate wealth and can repeat them over and over again.
- Build your finances using the magic of compound interest, tax-free accumulation and safe, positive leverage.
- Begin now to develop multiple streams of income: (1) earned income, (2) portfolio income, and (3) passive income; and understand how these three types of income are taxed.

LEARNING LINKS

Please visit www.MissedFortune.com/Millionaire-By-Thirty and click on the learning portal for chapter 3 to view various educational video streams that explain:

- The three marvels of wealth accumulation—lift, thrust, and drag
- The three lodging places for money (houses of straw, sticks, and bricks)
- The various stages or phases of financial maturity
- The three key elements of a prudent investment (the "LASER" test).

CHAPTER 4

Pay Yourself First

Budget, Save Money, and Manage Debt Properly—Live Within
Your Means

CHANCES ARE YOU'VE TRIED or at least noticed exercise tread-
mills at the gym. You climb onto a wide rubber belt and push
some buttons on the display in front of you to make the belt move.
It forces you to walk or run at a pace you set. But even after you
have exercised for a length of time and the electronic display in
front of you says you've gone three miles, a glance around the room
tells you that you have not moved from the same spot.

If you are already in the workforce, you may feel as though you
are on a financial treadmill. Perhaps you have signed up for "direct
deposit," so your paycheck is directly deposited into your checking
account. As a month starts, you write checks to pay regularly occur-
ring costs: the minimum amount required on your credit card state-
ments, rent, your electric and phone bills. When you need cash, you
get it from an ATM using a card connected to that same account.
Before long, what seemed like an ample amount of money dwindles
to almost nothing. You may even wind up using your credit card
to pay for your gas, movie tickets, and restaurant tabs until the end

of the pay period, when you know your checking account will be replenished.

Meanwhile, even though a period of time has passed, you are still in the same spot you were at—you don't have any money. You're back where you started, and the whole cycle starts again.

That's what we meant when we said earlier that some people find themselves with too much month left at the end of their money. These people are Strivers.

In this chapter we're going to show you a simple way to step off that treadmill so that you can truly move forward in accumulating money and become a Thriver. You'll learn a strategy that lets you live within your means. We'll teach you how to save money for important future purchases and also how to give some money away to charity.

In the previous chapter, we said there were three sources of income: people at work, money at work, and charity. If you are being compensated for providing services or goods, you're a person at work. Your goal should be to make the transition as quickly as possible from the "people at work" stage to the point when your money is also at work. Follow our plan, and in your thirties your money can be earning as much or more than you can. It all begins with basic discipline.

In keeping with our theme of threes, there are three attitudes young adults often have toward money:

1) Clueless
2) Carefree
3) Cautious

You know you're clueless if you cannot for the life of you figure out how the money from your last paycheck managed to disappear. Or perhaps you have an idea where the money went, but your attitude is, "There's more where that came from." In that case, you are carefree. Maybe you are the overly cautious type: You're discouraged at the thought that you must deprive yourself of the latte you buy every morning for the next forty years in order to save money.

Pay Yourself First, Then Pay Yourself Forward

Why do we think it is so crucial for you to live within your means in this era of multiple lines of credit and a "consumer society" obsessed with buying the latest thing? Because the lessons you learn as a young adult can stand you in good stead for the rest of your life. *One of the great secrets to wealth accumulation is to discipline yourself to live on no more than 80 percent of your net after-tax income. Allocate at least 20 percent of every dollar earned to pay yourself first and pay yourself forward.*

In fact for some inspirational advice on thrift and budgeting, you might well heed the lessons in *The Richest Man in Babylon*, by George S. Clason,* a book first published in 1926 that has been reprinted over and over and today is getting more attention than ever for its timeless wisdom.

Babylon was the wealthiest city in the ancient world. In the book, friends ask its richest citizen how, while he started no better off than they were, he attained his lofty status. His answers are a series of parables, or stories intended to convey a message. At the beginning he states his credo:

> A part of all you earn is yours to keep. It should be no less than a tenth, no matter how little you earn. It can be as much more as you can afford. *Pay yourself first.* Do not buy from the clothes-maker and the sandal maker more than you can pay out of the rest and still have enough for food and charity and penance to the gods. (emphasis added)

---

* George S. Clason, *The Richest Man in Babylon,* Signet reissue, 2004. Paperback, $6.99.

This wonderful book reminds us that throughout time, people will always be there with their hand out—from your landlord to your car dealer and so forth. That's why, no matter what you earn, you should take the first 10 percent of that and pay *yourself* by putting it into savings for both long-term and short-term rewards.

"Which desirest thou the most? Is it the gratification of thy desires of each day, a newel, a bit of finery. . . . Or is it substantial belongings, gold, land—income-bringing investments?" The answer, says the richest man, is that the "coins thou takest from thy purse bring the first. The coins thou leavest within it will bring the latter."

In that spirit, we suggest that the first move you should make financially each pay period is to sock away 10 percent of your income for later. Of that, at least 6 percent, or $60 for every $1,000 you make, is for *long-term* savings—meaning down the road, as well as retirement savings.

The remaining 4 percent is for short-term savings—for a car, a piano, a vacation, or something like that. When you start making more money, we recommend to many of our clients that they sock away 10 percent for long-term savings and another entire 10 percent for short-term savings, but that's hard for a lot of young people. The point is, don't wait until you have bought your first house, or until you reach a six-figure income or any other milestone you might have in your head.

Later on we hope to empower you so you can begin to save a total of 20 percent. And we will soon show you how much easier it is than you might think to find a total of 20 percent, and where the best place to put it may be. For now, all that matters is to keep the concept in mind.

That still leaves 10 percent out of each paycheck, or, as the richest man in Babylon would say, one coin out of your original ten. This money is what you should contribute to charity.

Some people call this paying yourself forward. Others call it giving back to the world, to society, to God. In our church, we teach it as tithing. It's one of the concepts that has helped not only me, but all of our six children. Ever since they were small, they were taught that from the money they earned mowing lawns or delivering newspapers or whatever, they should put 10 percent of it into charitable contributions. You might be thinking, "I can't afford this yet. I'm not making enough money." We would reply that you can't afford *not* to give 10 percent, because it has probably helped us each grow much more than the amount we gave up.

How to Build a Foolproof Beginner Budget

Josh: Aaron, I know I should keep better track of the money I spend, but the truth is, I just go to the ATM when I need cash— usually every Friday. And I also have five credit cards, because the banks and credit card companies keep sending me mailings that make it easy to get more than one card. Of course, they all have limits, but once I max out one card, I can always use another. Help! What should I do?

Aaron: It's not that hard, really. It starts with writing things down. I know how much I have because I keep running totals in my checking account. I try to avoid those tempting card offers we get in the mail because when you don't pay in full, you get slammed with a pretty high interest rate on the unpaid portion. I have a personal checking account, and I'll have a joint account with my wife when I'm married. As an entrepreneur, I have a business checking account too. I don't spend all the money that I make. I want to be sure that I live within my means. It'll just take a little discipline on your part, but I know you can do it.

We would like Aaron's friend Josh and all of you, whether you are clueless, carefree, or cautious, to consider our beginner budgeting system that allows you to physically understand how much money you have to spend and save. Right now, get yourself some envelopes. It's common to first think of larger categories, such as *food*, *clothing*, and *shelter*, so you might start labeling those. But remember, there are three categories we have already mentioned that cover at least the first 20 percent of your take-home pay. You should label envelopes or allow for them first:

- Short-term savings
- Long-term savings
- Charity

With a little thought, you might want to create a set of separate smaller envelopes to match specific expenses within larger categories, such as:

- In the larger *long-term savings* envelope, there might be smaller envelopes representing your 401(k), life insurance, and mutual funds.
- In the larger *short-term savings* envelope, there might be smaller envelopes representing your passbooks savings, furniture fund, and vacation fund.
- In the larger food envelope, there will be smaller envelopes for groceries, and perhaps for restaurant and take-out meals.
- In the *shelter or housing* envelope, you might have a smaller one for *rent* or, if you already own a house, *mortgage* payment, as well as others for utilities such as the *electricity* bill, your *phone* (whether it is a land line and/or cell), *heat*, *water and sewage*, and perhaps *trash* collection.
- Within *clothing* might be envelopes for *laundry and dry cleaning* as well as *new clothes* you buy.
- You will also need an envelope for *health and medical* expenses (*doctor/dentist visits*, *pharmacy needs*, *health insurance premiums*, etc.).

- Include one for *education* (*newspapers and magazines, tuition* if you are still in school, *Internet* connection, etc.).
- You will want an envelope for *transportation* expenses (*gas, commuting, parking, auto insurance,* and *taxes*—if you pay property taxes annually, just divide by 12).
- Of course you will need an envelope for *loans* (*car loan, student loan,* etc.).
- Don't forget envelopes for your *discretionary spending*: *entertainment* (this includes your *cable TV* bill; *movies* and/or *theater, club fees* or *shows, ball games* and *sports,* and other *events; sporting goods, music downloads, birthday* and *wedding presents,* etc).
- And you will need envelopes for each *credit card*.

Not everyone will need all these envelopes, and some people might add some. For example, in order to protect against uncertainty, everyone should make sure they have adequate health insurance. Also, if you are married and only one spouse is employed, even if you are not yet planning children, you should carry some life insurance. You may not think you need it, but it can provide for the dependent spouse in the unlikely event that the breadwinner passes away. Later, we'll show you how you can have adequate life insurance and have Uncle Sam help you pay for it.

For three months, I want you to withdraw 80 percent of your monthly take-home pay from your checking account and stash the actual cash in the various expense envelopes. (Or you can use plain-paper representations of that cash. You can download templates for "Missed Fortune Bucks" from www.MissedFortune.com/MissedFortuneBucks for this exercise.) If you are married and both spouses work, naturally you will pool money from both your jobs. Keep the envelopes in a safe location at home. You'll be tracking how much you spend on each category every month, and you'll use the real greenbacks to pay for each item.

The point of this budgeting exercise is to discover precisely what your spending habits are. Each time you withdraw money from an envelope to pay for something, note that expense on the outside of the envelope. Now, of course, in today's world, some items are not paid for in cash, such as the mortgage, health insurance, and so forth. And other items are set up for automatic withdrawal, such as your savings and investments. Where using cash is not feasible or possible, you may want to create some kind of voucher with the total for that expense, put it in the envelope, and write the total on the outside of the envelope. Feel free to use your own creativity to make this exercise work for you. And if there is an expense you forgot to make an envelope for, realize you will have to take money out of other envelopes to put in this new one.

Let's assume you have $3,050 per month to spend after tax. Figure 4.1 shows a sample of how much might be in each of the envelopes. The most important thing is, if an expense crops up and the envelope earmarked for it is empty, you'll have to make a sacrifice from another category.

What if you have budgeted $100 for entertainment and it is gone by the twentieth of the month—and then friends ask you to join them for dinner and a movie? You either take $30 or so out of the envelope marked "gas" or "clothing," or you say, "Sorry, but I've maxed out my entertainment budget for the month," and stay home.

It doesn't matter whether you are living at home, at school, or on your own. It doesn't matter whether you are single or married, have roommates or not, or are working full-time or part-time. The physical act of taking cash out of envelopes makes a dramatic impact on your view of living within your means.

When Sharee and I were first married years ago, we actually had a metal box in which we kept envelopes labeled for different expenses. We were attending college. I was working as a manager for a Kentucky Fried Chicken franchise, and Sharee was a sales clerk at a bookstore. We didn't have $3,000 a month—our income was quite a bit lower than that. But the amount is not the object of this

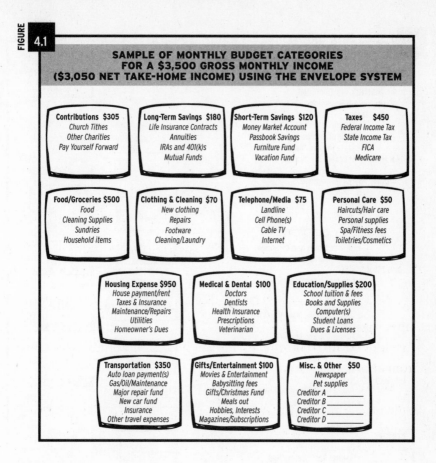

FIGURE 4.1

SAMPLE OF MONTHLY BUDGET CATEGORIES
FOR A $3,500 GROSS MONTHLY INCOME
($3,050 NET TAKE-HOME INCOME) USING THE ENVELOPE SYSTEM

Contributions $305
Church Tithes
Other Charities
Pay Yourself Forward

Long-Term Savings $180
Life Insurance Contracts
Annuities
IRAs and 401(k)s
Mutual Funds

Short-Term Savings $120
Money Market Account
Passbook Savings
Furniture Fund
Vacation Fund

Taxes $450
Federal Income Tax
State Income Tax
FICA
Medicare

Food/Groceries $500
Food
Cleaning Supplies
Sundries
Household items

Clothing & Cleaning $70
New clothing
Repairs
Footware
Cleaning/Laundry

Telephone/Media $75
Landline
Cell Phone(s)
Cable TV
Internet

Personal Care $50
Haircuts/Hair care
Personal supplies
Spa/Fitness fees
Toiletries/Cosmetics

Housing Expense $950
House payment/rent
Taxes & Insurance
Maintenance/Repairs
Utilities
Homeowner's Dues

Medical & Dental $100
Doctors
Dentists
Health Insurance
Prescriptions
Veterinarian

Education/Supplies $200
School tuition & fees
Books and Supplies
Computer(s)
Student Loans
Dues & Licenses

Transportation $350
Auto loan payment(s)
Gas/Oil/Maintenance
Major repair fund
New car fund
Insurance
Other travel expenses

Gifts/Entertainment $100
Movies & Entertainment
Babysitting fees
Gifts/Christmas Fund
Meals out
Hobbies, Interests
Magazines/Subscriptions

Misc. & Other $50
Newspaper
Pet supplies
Creditor A _____
Creditor B _____
Creditor C _____
Creditor D _____

lesson. When you experience how you have to sacrifice, learning the difference between a "want" versus a "need" can be extremely educational and revealing. It was almost painful back in those days to have this conversation:

"Is there any money left in that envelope, honey?"

"No."

"Well, we better tell our friends that we can't go, or else we'll have to forgo buying that new pair of jeans for you and those shoes for me."

Even doing this for only one month might be useful. When you realize you have to sacrifice something else in order to have some-

FIGURE 4.2

MISSED FORTUNE 101 BUDGETING TEMPLATE (SAMPLE)

TOTAL MONTHLY GROSS INCOME:		$ 3,500.00
Less Payroll Deductions:		
Taxes:		
• FICA/Medicare (7.65%)	$ 268.00	
• Federal Income Tax	$ (150.00)	
• State Income Tax	$ 32.00	
Total Monthly Net After-Tax Income:		
		$ 3,050.00
Other Payroll Deductions:		$ < 70.00 >
Health Insurance:	$ Employer Pays	
Savings:		
• 401(k)	$ 70.00	
• Other: _____	$	
Charitable Contributions:		$ 305.00 >
• Church Tithes and Offerings	$ 305.00	
• Other Charitable Causes	$	
LONG-TERM SAVINGS:		$ < 110.00 >
• Life Insurance Contracts	$ 110.00	
• Annuities	$	
• IRAs	$	
• Stocks, Bonds, Mutual Funds	$	
SHORT-TERM SAVINGS:		$ < 120.00 >
• Money Market Account	$	
• Passbook Savings	$ 40.00	
• Furniture Fund	$ 40.00	
• Vacation Fund	$ 40.00	
HOUSING EXPENSE:		$ < 870.00 >
• House payment (Principal and Interest)/Rent	$ 790.00	
• Taxes and Insurance	$ 80.00	
• Maintenance and Repairs	$	
• Homeowner's Dues	$	
UTILITIES:		$ < 80.00 >
• Power/Electricity	$ 40.00	
• Natural Gas/Heating Fuel	$ 30.00	
• Sewer	$ Included	
• Water	$ 10.00	
• Trash	$ Included	
FOOD/GROCERIES:		$ < 500.00 >
• Food	$ 430.00	
• Cleaning Supplies	$ 25.00	
• Sundries	$ 20.00	
• Household Items	$ 25.00	
• _____	$	
CLOTHING AND CLEANING:		$ 70.00 >
• New Clothing	$ 40.00	
• Dry Cleaning and Laundry	$ (5.00	
• Footwear_____	$ (5.00	
• Repairs & Mending	$	
• _____	$	
INSTALLMENT LOANS/CREDIT CARD DEBT: Balance:		$ < 30.00 >
Creditor A: Visa Credit Card $ 330.00	$ 30.00	
Creditor B: _____ $ _____	$	
Creditor C: _____ $ _____	$	
Creditor D: _____ $ _____	$	

MISSED FORTUNE 101 BUDGETING TEMPLATE (SAMPLE)

TRANSPORTATION EXPENSE: $ ‹ 350.00 ›
- Car Loan Payment $ 160.00
- Gas $ 100.00
- Oil and Maintenance $ 10.00
- Insurance (Monthly Equivalent) $ 40.00
- Other Travel Expense $
- Major Repair Fund $ 20.00
- New Car Fund $ 20.00

PERSONAL CARE: $ ‹ 50.00 ›
- Haircuts $ 30.00
- Toiletries/Cosmetics $ 10.00
- Spa/Fitness $
- Personal Supplies $ 10.00

MEDICAL & DENTAL: $ ‹ 100.00 ›
- Doctors $ 30.00
- Dentists $ 20.00
- Prescription Medicines $ 20.00
- Health Insurance Co-Pay $ 25.00
- Veterinarian $ 5.00

TELEPHONE AND MEDIA: $ ‹ 75.00 ›
- Landline $ 20.00
- Cell Phone(s) $ 30.00
- Internet $ 25.00
- Cable TV $

EDUCATION AND SUPPLIES: $ ‹ 200.00 ›
- Tuition & Fees $
- Student Loan Payment $ 150.00
- Computer $ 25.00
- Books and Supplies $ 25.00
- _____ $

GIFTS AND ENTERTAINMENT: $ ‹ 100.00 ›
- Movies/Theater/Video Rental $ 30.00
- Gifts and Christmas Fund $ 40.00
- Magazines and Subscriptions $
- Babysitting Expense $
- Meals Out $ 20.00
- Hobbies and Interests $
- Sports and Athletics $ 10.00

MISCELLANEOUS AND OTHER EXPENSES: $ ‹ 20.00 ›
- Newspaper $ 10.00
- Pet Supplies $ 10.00
- _____ $

TOTAL EXPENSES: $ 3,050.00
BUDGET BALANCE: (Surplus or Shortage) $ BALANCED

thing you really want or need, then it's easier to turn down people and say, "Next time. Right now, we really can't afford it."

How to Build an Intermediate or Advanced Budget

Amanda: Now that we're in the twenty-first century, Emron, your dad's envelope system sounds a little on the old-fashioned side!

Emron: You may be right, but we could definitely do the same thing with a spreadsheet or software system. The principles are the same.

A lot of people may not want to go to the extreme of separating cash or vouchers into envelopes, although when they do it's a big wake-up call. If you are not totally clueless and you think you can manage with a less old-fashioned method, there are two alternative budgeting systems.

Intermediate Method

This uses the same idea as envelopes, except you don't have to use cash. Instead, open up several checking accounts earmarked for major categories of expenses. Thus you have a checking account for *shelter* and related costs; another for *food, clothing,* and *transportation;* another for *entertainment* and *gifts;* and another for *loan* or *credit card payments.* You will experience the same discomfort when one checkbook is nearly empty, even when using checks instead of cash.

Aaron uses one business and several personal checking accounts. Emron and his wife, Harmony, have one checking account for most expenses, another specifically for car payments.

Advanced Method

Once Sharee and I had tried out the envelope system for a few months, we switched to a ledger.

Alternatively, you may find it simpler and more in keeping with your technological orientation to use personal finance software such as Quicken or Microsoft Money.* They cost only about $30 and you can download a copy directly from each company's Web site. (You can even download a portable one to your Palm or BlackBerry, so you can enter amounts as soon as you pay for something.)

Whether you use a ledger (a set of 8½-by-11 sheets of ruled paper), a spreadsheet, or a software program, simply create the categories you need and manage all of them under a single checking account. In this way, you can keep a running balance of how much money you have left in each category by looking at your bottom line.

LINK TIP: Go to www.MissedFortune.com/Millionaire-By-Thirty, and under the learning portal for chapter 4 you can find a blank template of the budget sheet. Also you can print templates of envelopes and Missed Fortune Bucks for your envelopes. Or simply download a spreadsheet that can help you track your budgeting with different categories.

What About Credit Cards?

As Emron tells his younger clients, "Use your credit card as a tool." Credit cards still have to be subject to your monthly budget, and most certainly *not* to the full extent of credit a card issuer grants you. That limit could be as high as $10,000, and if you start amassing that kind of debt you'll find yourself in a very deep hole. *You should control your credit cards; they should not control you.*

Keep in mind when using credit cards that this is not free money. Card issuers are eager to sign you up because many young adults do not pay the full amount shown on their statement each month. Rather, they pay the minimum, which can be as little as $10. On every other dollar remaining, you will be paying interest

---

* http://personal-finance-software-review.toptenreviews.com/. This Web site indicates that Quicken and MS Money are the top two kinds.

that might be 10, 12, or even as high as 18 to 26 percent. If you take money from an ATM using your credit card, you'll be charged a higher rate of interest on that cash than you are charged when you buy goods or services.

Yes, there are advantages to credit cards. Young adults typically do not have a credit history when they start their first full-time jobs, and a good credit history is important for getting the best rates on mortgages and any other kind of loan except student loans. *So while we still recommend having credit cards, we urge absolute caution and self-control with them.*

Build a Great Credit History

Once you have your first credit card, be careful about making at least the minimum payment each month to avoid tarnishing your credit history. This credit history is based on your record as a bill payer. It also is affected by the number and types of credit cards and loans you have, collection actions, outstanding debt, and the age of your accounts.

It is simple these days to learn what your "credit score" is, and that's something you should check once a year. Your credit score is determined by a company called Fair Isaac Corporation (FICO).* The highest score possible is 850. Aim to keep your score at 720 or higher to get the best deals on mortgage rates and other credit. Three credit reporting companies—Equifax, Experian, and Trans-Union—each compile a credit score on you. They are not necessarily identical. These agencies look into such things as paying your home mortgage on time, making regular payments on such installment plans as your car loan, retail store accounts, and the like. Federal law says you are entitled to request and get a free report from each reporting company every twelve months. You can learn more

---

* http://www.myfico.com/CreditEducation/.

about how to obtain your scores at www.annualcreditreport.com. It is crucial to correct any mistakes.

Unfortunately, understanding all of the ways that your credit score can be affected is almost a secret. For a moment imagine: You are competing in the Olympic tryouts. The three judges determining your score will display it for onlookers by holding a scorecard. You ask in advance what criteria the judges will use to rate your performance. Instead of explaining the technical merits upon which you will be scored, the judges simply give you a hint or two, leaving you guessing and uncertain.

You are shocked to learn that you received three very different scores: one high, one mediocre, and one low. The high and low scores cancel each other out, and you are left with a mediocre score, hardly enough to pass to the next round. You wonder why the scores are conflicting. Frustrated, you hope for a shot in the next Olympic tryouts, but without feedback, you fear you will not make the cut.

In the world of credit scoring, the rules are confusing, constantly changing, and often unavailable to the general public. Unable to get a handle on the rules of the game, borrowers pay high interest rates or, worse yet, fail to qualify for loans. Because of the complexity of the system, consumers across the board feel confused, isolated, and powerless. They usually feel that they have nowhere to turn, and they panic when they realize the extreme adverse affects of negative credit.

The word "score" is usually associated with a number that expresses accomplishment or excellence as compared to a previously established standard. Your score in a sport is determined by how well you play the game, the rules of which are defined in advance. In a test, your score is a reflection of how well you know the material previously made available.

To establish and maintain an excellent credit score, it is best to:

- Pay all of your accounts on a timely basis every month

- Keep your credit card balances under 30 percent of your credit limit
- Have at least three revolving credit lines (balances that can be carried over from one month to the next) that you pay on time *and* pay off regularly
- Have at least one timely paid active installment loan or a paid installment loan on your credit report

A credit score of 720 or higher can qualify a person for the best mortgage interest rates when borrowing for a home. A difference of 2 percent better interest on a $180,000 mortgage loan (or a difference of 1 percent better interest on a $360,000 mortgage) can save a borrower $300 per month in interest. If that $300 of otherwise payable interest were saved each month in an investment earning an average rate of return of 8.5 percent over a thirty-year period, it would grow to nearly half a million dollars!

For more on credit scores, I suggest you look at my friend Philip Tirone's book *7 Steps to a 720 Credit Score*. He teaches people how to win the credit game. The book will also show you how to turn poor credit into great credit, a move that can save you hundreds of dollars a month by qualifying for a lower interest rate on a mortgage and/or home equity line of credit.

Be Wary of the Hard Sell on New Credit Cards

When you have built up a good credit history, you can look into applying for a credit card that charges as little as zero percent for the first several months, or when you transfer balances from a previous credit card. *But beware of reading just the percentage*; that zero percent is never offered on everything forever. It's usually an enticement, an introductory rate to encourage you to move your purchases to that credit card issuer.

Most credit cards should really be viewed almost as debit cards. That is, if you don't have the money, you shouldn't be using the card. It is simply a convenience, a place where you can consolidate payments so you only have to fill out one check for a variety of items or expenses. In our family, we usually use credit cards for gasoline and transportation if we are traveling. Yes, if it's December we might use a credit card to buy things for Christmas, and this is a good way to keep track of Christmas expenses. But we don't want to be paying for Christmas until June of the following year.

What's more, the interest that you pay on credit card balances that you allow to carry over from one month to the next (revolving accounts) is, more often than not, money that you are tossing out the window. It is what we call nonpreferred interest, or money that has no value as a tax deduction. That's in contrast to the interest you pay on a mortgage when you buy a house, which is preferred interest. It is deductible on your federal income tax return, a gift from Uncle Sam. We go into this in detail in upcoming chapters.

What If You Are Buried in Nonpreferred Debt Already?

Sometimes it may behoove a person to exchange nonpreferred debt for preferred debt. This means that rather than paying 18 percent interest in nondeductible interest on credit card balances, it might be in your best interest to consolidate that debt using a home equity line of credit. But beware, by doing so, you are borrowing to consume rather than to conserve. However, if you save the difference in payments and discipline yourself to not run up your credit card balances again, it can be a smart strategy. Why?

Let's say a home equity line charges 10 percent interest. But because it is tax-deductible, it may only cost you a net of 8 percent in a 20 percent tax bracket, as you'll learn later. You would, in effect, be trading 18 percent for 8 percent interest, which results in a savings of 10 percent in interest (which equals $100 a year for every $1,000 you owe)—a wise move. But when consolidating debt, it is imperative that you set up a system and discipline yourself to save the difference in payments into your saving and investment side fund that we will introduce later. In other words, don't free up monthly cash flow by lowering your payments and then use the cash to consume.

If you are heavily in debt, you must set up your budgeting system so that you can manage the debt and make the monthly payments necessary to meet your obligations in a responsible and accountable manner with the resources you have. When there is more outgo than income, you either need to decrease your monthly outgo or increase your monthly income—or do both. If you cannot meet the minimum monthly payments, communicate with your creditors and negotiate a workable payment plan. Demonstrate your desire and willingness to pay your obligations. You'll find that goodwill and telling the truth will go a long way toward your progress in getting out of debt. As you pay off one creditor, allocate that monthly outlay (which you are already used to shelling out) to the next creditor. Pay off creditors charging the highest interest rate first. Attack your debt with serious vigor. But remember that you must still pay yourself first every month by saving something, even if it is a small amount. I have witnessed many people who allocated every dollar they had to retiring all debt as soon as possible, only to find themselves with no liquidity (ability to access money) when they really needed it for an emergency such as an accident, temporary illness, or unemployment. So, it is wise to save some of your money while you are paying off nonpreferred debt. The goal is to have interest working for you rather than against you as soon as possible.

What to Do About Student Loans

A lot of you who have recently left college will likely regard the money you still owe on student loans as your most serious debt. The fact is that student loans are not the worst kind of debt to have. While you are still in school, payments on those loans are deferred.

Once you are out of school, you have a six-month grace period before you must begin to start repaying the money.

Naturally, you should not ignore them completely. But the interest rate on those loans is relatively low—as of this writing, federal student loan interest is about 7 percent, and some states will offer you lower rates if you have attended a state college or university and you reside in that state.

The biggest mistake some young adults make is trying to accelerate payments in order to wipe student loans off the books. Emron has created the chart below to show you that there are two ways to pay your student loans—the traditional way, and the "millionaire way."

FIGURE 4.3

ACCELERATING PAYOFF OF A STUDENT LOAN TRADITIONAL WAY VERSUS THE MILLIONAIRE WAY

Loan Amount	$20,000		Side Fund Rate	8%
Payment	$232.22		Extra Payment	$150
Term (Years)	10			
Interest Rate	7%			

Applying the $150 per month to loan   *Applying the $150 per month to a side fund*

Year	Student Loan Balance	Tax Savings	*Investment Balance	VERSUS	Student Loan Balance	Tax Savings	*Investment Balance	Annual Liquidity Difference
1	$16,709.15	$263.08	$274.76		$18,568.03	$270.93	$2,162.90	$1,888.14
2	$13,180.39	$224.46	$531.99		$17,032.55	$250.22	$4,483.69	$3,951.71
3	$9,396.55	$183.04	$767.31		$15,386.07	$228.02	$6,973.93	$6,206.61
4	$5,339.17	$138.64	$975.79		$13,620.56	$204.22	$9,645.99	$8,670.19
5	$988.48	$91.02	$1,151.85		$11,727.42	$178.69	$12,513.17	$11,361.32
6	$0.00	$39.96	$5,003.42		$9,697.43	$151.32	$15,589.73	$10,586.31
7	$0.00	$0.00	$10,209.00		$7,520.69	$121.97	$18,891.00	$8,682.00
8	$0.00	$0.00	$15,846.64		$5,186.59	$90.50	$22,433.41	$6,586.76
9	$0.00	$0.00	$21,952.20		$2,683.76	$56.75	$26,234.58	$4,282.38
10	$0.00	$0.00	$28,564.52		$0.00	$20.57	$30,313.46	$1,748.94

* Investment balance also reflects investing the tax savings.

In both examples shown, the amount of the loan to be repaid is $20,000. The repayment period is ten years (which is typical), and in both these cases the interest rate is 7 percent. Thus the amount owed is $232.22 each month for the next ten years (twelve payments a year for ten years equals 120 payments). However, Joe College, as we'll call the traditional payer (the left side in Emron's chart), tacks on an extra $150 a month in order to wipe out the debt faster.

At first it looks like the Joe College system might be better— nearly cutting in half the time to pay off the loan. He is all paid up. He has sent off a total of just under $24,000 to the loan company. But in the meantime, he has very little liquidity.

In contrast, Moe Millionaire, using the millionaire way, has paid almost $3,500 more after ten years, when he finally wipes the loan off the books.

But Moe Millionaire took his extra $150 and put it into a conservative investment side fund (we'll explain what these are a bit later on) that earned *him* 8 percent interest. After five years, he has more than $12,500 in liquid cash available. He could keep that invested, or use some of it in the event of an emergency rather than charging a high-interest credit card. After ten years, combining his extra $150 and the interest it earns, his side fund (which he plans to use as a retirement savings plan) has $30,313 in it.

Meanwhile, Joe College paid off his student loan in 5.2 years. He then put the extra $150 plus the amount he had been sending to the loan company ($232.22) into a similar side fund for the remaining 4.8 years (assuming he didn't have any unexpected expenses arise).

After ten years, Joe College's investment account still fell nearly $1,750 short of Moe Millionaire's. But Moe Millionaire had choice and control during the ten-year period rather than being at the mercy of banks and creditors until his loan was paid off.

The message here is, *pay yourself first*. Don't exhaust your extra resources helping the bank before you start helping yourself.

Uncle Sam's Tax Breaks on Student Loans

In chapter 5 we'll talk about tax deductions and exemptions. One of your key deductions may be the interest on your student

loans. The government thinks education is important and thus permits you a legitimate tax break on the interest you pay on money
borrowed for education, as well as the cost of tuition and fees. If
you paid $600 or more of interest on a qualified student loan during
the year, you will receive a Form 1098–E, or Student Loan Interest
Statement, from the financial institution (or any other person or
place to whom you had paid student loan interest).

In 2006, the interest deduction on student loans was either
$2,500 or the actual amount of interest, depending on which num-
ber was smaller. However, this amount might be gradually reduced
or eliminated based on your filing status and modified adjusted gross
income. In 2006, if you were single, your modified adjusted gross
income would have to be less than $50,000. If you were married
and filing a joint return, it would have to be less than $105,000.

Be sure to consult an experienced tax preparer on questions of
what kind of student loan interest and related educational costs you
are allowed to deduct from your federal tax return.

Saving for Long-Term Goals

Thus we return to the 10 percent of your income that you
should sock away for long-term goals. One easy way to start saving
is through your employer's 401(k) plan. Many employers offer to
match the amount that you put into this investment program up to
a certain amount. Those matching dollars *are* free money.

By all means sign up for the plan. But—and this is a big but—*we
suggest only contributing up to the amount required to receive the maximum match.* Why? Because we are going to show you better ways to
put the rest of your savings dollars to work for you. We will teach
you how you can make those dollars work so hard that by your thirties, your money can be earning more than you are. That's what we
mean by "money at work," as opposed to "people at work."

By now you may be wondering if one of the long-term goals you
are saving for is the down payment on a home. The answer is, no!

You don't have to wait any longer to buy a home, and you don't need a big sum as a down payment. In fact, the millionaire mindset is that you should not rent for any longer than absolutely necessary. In chapter 6, we will show you how you can use essentially the same amount of money you now spend on rent to buy your first home.

What about income tax? If you are working for a company, you will never see the money that goes to pay some of your income tax. *That's the withholding*—the amount taken out of your paycheck automatically by a firm and sent to Uncle Sam to cover your taxes. In the next chapter, we'll tell you all about the mistake that costs taxpayers thousands of dollars, how you can avoid it, and how you can put some legitimate tax breaks to work for you.

Remember, the most important concepts you can focus on now are learning to track your expenses, living within your means, paying yourself first, and even paying yourself forward.

REMEMBER THIS

- Take control of your money before it takes control of you by budgeting, saving money, managing debt properly, and living within your means.
- Pay yourself first and pay yourself forward even before paying off your nonpreferred debt—thus having interest work for you rather than against you.
- You can learn foolproof budgeting by setting aside real cash or Missed Fortune Bucks in envelopes marked for each kind of monthly expense—rent/mortgage, groceries, transportation, entertainment, and so forth.
- Learn to live on 80 percent of your take-home pay and allocate the first 20 percent of your earnings to savings and charity.
- Build a 720–plus credit score by paying at least the minimum on your credit cards each month, paying off your revolving accounts periodically, keeping your credit card balances under 30 percent of your credit limit, and getting a free credit report once a year.
- Only use home equity debt consolidation loans when you have a system that will keep you disciplined to set aside the difference in payments into savings or paying off the debt sooner rather than spending the difference.

LEARNING LINKS

Visit www.MissedFortune.com/Millionaire-By-Thrity and click on the learning portal for chapter 4 to:
- Download a lengthy, detailed list of money-saving tips that can save you thousands of dollars over time and free up money to save and invest.

- Download a blank template of the Missed Fortune 101 Budgeting Worksheet and templates of the envelopes and Missed Fortune Bucks for the envelopes as well as a spreadsheet that can help you track your budgeting.
- Download a free booklet containing thirty-eight important facts about credit titled "I'll Bet You Didn't Know This About Credit" by Philip Tirone.
- Order Philip Tirone's book *7 Steps to a 720 Credit Score* at a discounted price.

CHAPTER 5

Don't Give Uncle Sam Gifts

Understand Taxes and How to Leverage Otherwise Payable
Income Tax

ARE YOU A MEMBER OF UNCLE SAM'S Christmas Club?
For much of the last century, the Christmas Club was a
popular plan offered by many savings institutions. When you joined
the club, you gave the bank the authorization to automatically
transfer a sum of money each week or month from your checking
account to a club savings account. Banks paid little or no interest
on these club accounts, but they would deliver the total amount
in a lump sum to you at a certain time each year. People used the
Christmas Club because it forced them to anticipate the need for
money to cover the expenses of gifts or a vacation.

Millions of young Americans today make the mistake of opening the equivalent of Christmas Club accounts with the Internal
Revenue Service. Either deliberately or through oversight, they
allow their employers to allocate too much money in withholding
tax each month. That money goes to the IRS to cover their April
tax bill. When these taxpayers actually prepare their taxes, they discover they've overpaid, and they get a refund. "Isn't this great!"

they exclaim. "I'm getting a tax refund of $2,500, and I'm going to use it to splurge on a weekend in the Caribbean."

This is one of the three most common mistakes that taxpayers make. They lose the use of thousands of dollars by withholding too much from their paychecks. We are going to show you how to avoid this one, and how to capitalize on correcting two other big mistakes.

If you are one of those people who gets a refund each year because you've overpaid your taxes, think about it this way: When *you owe the government* taxes, Uncle Sam *charges you interest* and penalties dating back to the time you should have paid them. But when the government owes *you* a return on your overpaid taxes (because your extra withholding has essentially been depositing money in a Christmas Club account each month!), *how much extra* does Uncle Sam pay in interest on your refund?

Nothing. Nada.

If we've just described your situation, we urge you to call your employer's benefits office right away and say that you want to adjust the withholding on your paycheck. When you first went to work, you filled out a W-4 worksheet (Employee's Withholding Allowance Certificate) where you calculated how many exemptions you should claim on your taxes. That determines how much money is withheld, and it shows up when you get a W-2 form (your statement of wages and earnings that employers are required to send you by January 31 every year).

You may think that you can claim only as many exemptions as there are dependents in your household, including yourself. Not so! If too much money is being withheld—so much that you get an income tax refund each year—tell your employer you wish to fill out a new W-4 worksheet.

The worksheet is simply a guide. In 2007, taxpayers were allowed an exemption of $3,400 per dependent, or $6,800 for a married couple filing jointly. That's a portion of your income that is not subject to tax. But you can *claim as many exemptions as you need* to avoid unnecessary tax being collected that would be refunded to you upon filing your tax return. The number of exemptions you claim for withholding purposes can be totally different from the actual exemptions you claim on your 1040 tax return.

Act now to bring your withholding more in line with what your actual taxes will be. Then, presto! Your paycheck will be larger.

This does not mean you should spend the extra dollars. Right there is money you can use to start a millionaire mindset savings plan. (We recommend you deposit it in a side fund that we'll talk about soon.) This is the first way in which you can free up money and put it to work for you earning interest—rather than letting Uncle Sam hold it for you, where it doesn't earn any interest. This is not a loophole, and it does not make you a tax cheat. It makes you tax-smart.

A word of care: Before changing the exemptions on your withholding, it is best to meet with a personnel manager and hypothetically enter in different numbers of exemptions to see how your withholding tax will be reduced. *This is so you will not underestimate the amount you should be paying and owe too much tax at year's end.*

LINK TIP: For a simple calculator to help you determine how many exemptions you could claim on your W-4, go to the exemptions calculator found in the learning portal at www. MissedFortune.com/Millionaire-By-Thirty.

Jet-Propelled Savings

In chapter 3, we mentioned the three marvels of wealth accumulation. The first, you'll recall, is the magic of compound interest. Similar to the same powerful force that helps a kite fly and propels a jetliner off the tarmac, compound interest can give your finances a jet-propelled lift. So, take the extra money you have in each paycheck when you stop depositing it in Uncle Sam's Christmas Club account, and put it temporarily into a high-yield savings account, preferably in one where the interest is compounded *daily*. Rates are usually quoted as an annual percentage rate.

Perhaps you're thinking that it won't be a great deal of money. "I'm only saving $100 a month now!" If you look at figure 5.1, you'll see that $100 a month compounding for the next ten years at 8 percent interest mushrooms into $18,417 a decade from now.

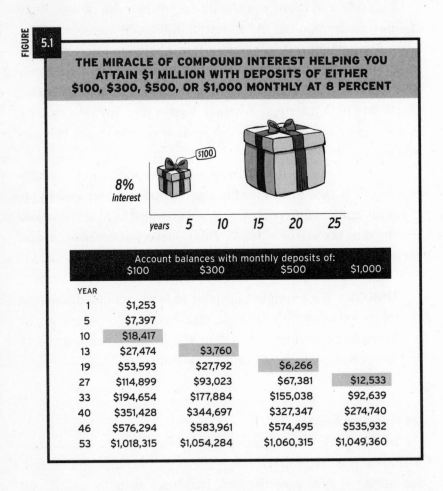

FIGURE 5.1

THE MIRACLE OF COMPOUND INTEREST HELPING YOU ATTAIN $1 MILLION WITH DEPOSITS OF EITHER $100, $300, $500, OR $1,000 MONTHLY AT 8 PERCENT

8% interest

years   5   10   15   20   25

| YEAR | Account balances with monthly deposits of: | | | |
	$100	$300	$500	$1,000
1	$1,253			
5	$7,397			
10	$18,417			
13	$27,474	$3,760		
19	$53,593	$27,792	$6,266	
27	$114,899	$93,023	$67,381	$12,533
33	$194,654	$177,884	$155,038	$92,639
40	$351,428	$344,697	$327,347	$274,740
46	$576,294	$583,961	$574,495	$535,932
53	$1,018,315	$1,054,284	$1,060,315	$1,049,360

If you're a twenty-five-year-old, making this small correction in your withholding puts you in position for a jet-propelled Christmas Club savings by your thirty-fifth birthday! At that point in time, if you were to stop depositing $100 per month and just let your savings balance of $18,417 grow at 8 percent, it would blossom into $185,324 over the next thirty years to age sixty-five (ten times as much).

In figure 5.1, notice that $100 invested per month at 8 percent interest grows to more than $1 million in fifty-three years. But it requires a monthly investment of $1,000 (ten times as much) when you have half as much time to accomplish your goal of $1 million. The lesson?—*the longer you wait to begin saving and investing, the more you will need to set aside to achieve your goals.*

Compounding is one of the marvels of the universe. Contrary to simple interest earnings where you only earn the same amount of interest each year on the original principal balance, compound interest allows you to earn interest each year on your principal *and* accumulated interest. For example, if you could set aside $10,000 for your newborn baby in an account that was crediting 7.2 percent simple interest, the account would credit $720 each year. When your child turned age sixty-seven, the account would have earned $720 a year for sixty-seven years, bringing the total account value to $58,240. How does that compare to compound interest?

The "Rule of 72" tells us that at a given interest rate, if you divide that rate into 72, the result indicates how many years it will take to double your money when it is compounding. For example, if you earned 8 percent compound interest, your money would double every 9 years (72 divided by 8 equals 9); if you earned 10 percent compound interest, your money would double every 7.2 years. So in the above example, $10,000 growing at 7.2 interest compounded annually would mean your account balance would double in value about every 10 years. The same account with $10,000 growing at 7.2 percent interest *compounding annually* would blossom to $1,054,510 by the time your child turned sixty-seven—over 18 times the amount that simple interest produced.

In my previous books *Missed Fortune* and *Missed Fortune 101*, I illustrate that a dollar doubling every period for twenty periods will grow to more than $1 million. In *The Last Chance Millionaire*, I illustrate that if you could fold a normal sheet of copy paper (26 lb. paper) in half fifty times, thus doubling its thickness each time, the stack of paper would be over ninety-three million miles high (from here to the sun)—because the thickness of the paper would have doubled fifty times. If you could double it one more time—fifty-one times—the stack would reach from here to the sun and back! That's the magic of compounding! This is the same math that takes a single female cell (the oocyte), which is about 35 microns in diameter when it is fertilized by the male cell (the spermatozoan), which is only about 3 microns in diameter, and causes it to split, double, and grow countless times to develop into a human being—the magnitude of which can be approximated as ten trillion cells in nine months and as many as one hundred trillion cells in an adult.

Marginal or Effective Tax Bracket?

Our goal is to help you also accumulate money in a tax-free environment. In order to understand other strategies, we need to explain a bit about some dry subjects: income tax forms and "marginal" versus "effective" tax brackets. These are other "orange rinds"—once we get through the not-so-tasty part, the rewards will be sweet.

When you prepare your taxes, you have a choice to claim a "standard deduction." In 2007, this was $5,350 for a single person or $10,700 for a married couple filing jointly. If you make this choice, you send the IRS the short income tax form called the 1040EZ. But there is another way to file your taxes where you itemize your deductions: the longer 1040 form.

If you make less than $20,000 a year, you automatically fall into the lowest of six tax brackets. In this situation, you get the standard deduction of $5,350 and you can claim a personal exemption of $3,400. Thus you are taxed on only $11,250 ($20,000 minus $8,750 equals $11,250). In this case, you probably don't need to itemize deductions, and you can use the EZ form.

But taxes get trickier once you make a better salary, or once you are married and both you and your spouse have jobs.

Let's say you are married and earned $50,000 in a year, and you paid roughly $4,000 in federal taxes. You may think, "Wow, that's only 8 percent." In reality, you probably paid 10 percent on about the first $16,000 of that salary. On every dollar over that "threshold," up to your "taxable income" (after deductions and exemptions are subtracted from your gross income of $50,000), you're paying more like 15 percent. Assuming you owned a home and had mortgage interest deductions as well as property tax deductions, in addition to charitable contribution deductions and personal exemptions, you may only end up with a taxable income of about $30,000.

Understand that the additional $34,000 (above the first $16,000 of earnings) puts you into a higher "marginal" tax bracket—15 percent in this case. That's the tax bracket that your last dollars earned put you into. Your "effective" tax bracket is the percentage rate you pay compared to your total income. So in this case—earning $50,000—your effective tax bracket was only 8 percent.

When we analyze the benefit of certain tax deductions, we calculate it using your *marginal* tax rate, rather than the *effective* tax rate. Why? Because it reflects the true tax savings you achieve from a deduction. You can keep the two kinds of brackets straight in your head by thinking of the *marginal* bracket as the more *meaningful* and *memorable* one. As you are about to see, it makes sense to itemize deductions when you are able to take advantage of legitimate tax breaks that Uncle Sam offers you.

Don't Make the Mistake of Filing a Short Income Tax Form

We said before that in tax year 2007 you got a flat $5,350 deduction as a single taxpayer using the short form of the federal IRS return, or $10,700 if you are married and you and your spouse are filing jointly. These deduction amounts are adjusted upwardly by the IRS about 3 or 4 percent each year. You may be tempted to spend as little time as possible on preparing your taxes and just fill out the short IRS return, which is called the 1040EZ.

But there are good reasons why you may want to file the longer form of the 1040 return. That's because on Schedule A of this return, you can claim deductions that might go considerably beyond these amounts.

The most meaningful deduction is one you may not be entitled to yet if you rent rather than own your own home. *Because the government thinks it is better to own a home than to rent one, the IRS allows you to deduct the interest on your first and second mortgages.* That's just one reason why we believe that the sooner you buy a home, the better off you will be. We'll explain more later, but suffice it to say for now that we recommend you buy a home as early in your adult life as you can, so you can begin deducting mortgage interest.

To illustrate, if you itemized the deductions on your most recent federal tax return, pull it out of your files and look at Schedule A.

Notice that by going to the trouble of filling out a long-form IRS return, you also can deduct such things as:

- State and local income taxes or sales tax
- Property taxes
- Charitable contributions
- Casualty and theft losses
- Tax preparation fees and the fees you pay your investment advisor, if you have one

Thus, for example, when you give back 10 percent of your income to charity, you are also allowed a legitimate tax break. Instead of giving money for government programs and letting the government decide how to spend that money, you are giving your money to specific causes you support.

If you have never filed a form like this, you will be amazed. The total amount of itemized deductions can be thousands of dollars higher than the $5,350 (for 2007) you are entitled to claim as a standard deduction. That reduces the amount of taxes you pay. We'll show how to take that money that you save on legitimate tax breaks and put it to work in a savings plan that will accumulate fast enough so that by the time you are in your thirties those savings will be earning more than you earn at your job.

Too often people say, "Aw, I don't want to put in the time to do my taxes." But think about it. Sometimes we'll get excited about getting a raise of one or two dollars an hour, or we'll work overtime for extra money. Then when it comes time to spend one to three hours filling out an income tax form, people don't want to spend the energy, time, or money. But you can actually *make* the equivalent of $500 an hour spending the extra time and energy (and perhaps fee) on taxes.

How Compound Interest Accelerates Your Wealth

Have you ever had a puppy or a kitten as a pet? Have you taken photos of the little animal? Compare those photos to what your pet looks like now, when he or she is all grown up. It's remarkable how quickly precious things in comparatively small packages grow, almost before your eyes.

Now imagine that you get your hands not on just $100 but on $100,000—money that you do not need right at this moment. We'll show you how almost right before your eyes—through the marvel of compound interest explained earlier—that amount can grow at just 6 percent into almost $180,000 in ten years.

Now imagine that you are planting a sapling in your backyard. That sapling will grow into a mighty tree in twenty years. In the same way, the $100,000 we are talking about might be able to grow at 7 or 8 percent. If that is the case, it will become $196,715 or $215,893 in ten years. That's how big your savings can grow.

It's the difference between a sapling and a huge elm or spruce— or the difference between a kite flying above your head and a jetliner zooming off a runway. This is savings that you can use to live on in the event of an unforeseen event like corporate downsizing or some other setback. Or it can be money that you use way down the road when you "retire."

Here's another point about the magic of compound interest. Some people think that if they have all their savings in one account, it will grow to a larger sum via compound interest than if they put the money in ten different accounts. That is not true. More money in one pot doesn't grow any faster than the same amount divided into several accounts growing at the same interest rate.

Keep this in mind for later on, when we talk about splitting retirement or savings funds and keeping them in a variety of places. Compounding makes the difference, not how big each individual sum is.

The Magic of Tax-Free Accumulation

We will show a little later how to enhance your wealth even more dramatically by letting it build up and earn compound interest in a streamlined, tax-free environment.

For now, let's consider the likelihood that taxes will continue to increase. When we ask audiences whether they expect taxes to go up, go down, or stay the same, most people believe taxes will only go up. That's another reason it makes so much sense to invest in an environment where you do not have to pay taxes later.

Please glance at figure 5.2, which depicts three of the four stages of saving for the long term. The four phases are:

1) Contribution
2) Accumulation
3) Distribution
4) Transfer. Since "transfer" is the money you transfer to your heirs upon your death (and hopefully that's a long way off), in keeping with our "power of threes" philosophy, we have not included it in the diagram.

You can make those savings grow in a tax-free rather than tax-deferred environment. Then you can not only contribute and accumulate money that is tax-favored, you can also draw on it (that's the "distribution" phase) at any age in a tax-free environment. That's the quicker road to financial independence.

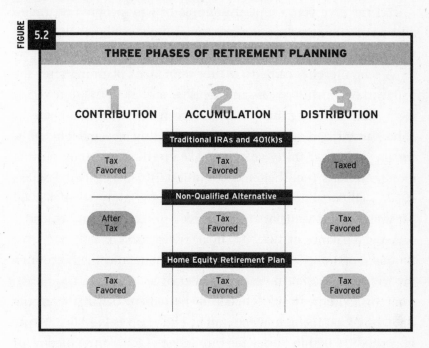

FIGURE 5.2

THREE PHASES OF RETIREMENT PLANNING

1 CONTRIBUTION	2 ACCUMULATION	3 DISTRIBUTION
Traditional IRAs and 401(k)s		
Tax Favored	Tax Favored	Taxed
Non-Qualified Alternative		
After Tax	Tax Favored	Tax Favored
Home Equity Retirement Plan		
Tax Favored	Tax Favored	Tax Favored

How much of a difference can it make to save in a tax-free environment, rather than pay taxes—even on the final phases? If you get 100–cent dollars on both the front and the back end of the first three phases, you could enjoy 50 percent more spendable retirement income. And because compound interest makes money grow more the longer you let it accumulate, right now, while you are young, is the best time to learn how to save without a tax liability lurking in the background.

Why You Should Be Wary of "Qualified" Retirement Plans

Your parents or grandparents can undoubtedly tell you how dis-illusioning it is to save money in a "tax-deferred" account, only to see Uncle Sam snatch back his gift to you once you draw on that money as a retiree.

Let me give you a typical example of why people find them-selves at retirement in a tax bracket as high or higher than they were in during their earning years.

A schoolteacher came to me for retirement planning after she had worked for thirty years and kept her money in the state retire-ment fund. Knowing that she would receive only about 60 percent of her earned income from the state in monthly retirement benefits, she prepared over thirty years to make up the shortfall by putting money in TSAs (tax-sheltered annuities), 403(b)s, and the state's 401(k)—all "qualified" plans. She had socked away about $3,000 per year in these vehicles at an average 8 percent return, which re-sulted in a balance of $375,000 by her retirement date.

Based on interest-only withdrawals from her qualified accounts, she will have $30,000 a year (8 percent of $375,000) of taxable in-come in addition to the $36,000 of retirement benefits from the state. Her total income in retirement ended up being $66,000 per year plus $16,000 in Social Security income, for a gross income of $82,000.

Sounds pretty good, right? What didn't sound so good were the looming taxes she would be clobbered with because she had paid off the mortgage on her home and had no dependents. She was shocked that her retirement tax bracket was actually greater than during her earning years.

Make no mistake, "tax-deferred" does not mean the same thing as "tax-free." The most popular so-called "qualified retirement plans" promoted by your employer, financial institutions, and giant mutual funds allow the tax on your savings in such plans as a 401(k), 403(b), IRA, or several others to be tax-favored *only when you contribute the money—and as the money accumulates*. Indeed, "qualified" means that you are contributing to plans considered "qualified" according to Uncle Sam's rules.

Retirement plans are simply long-term savings plans. Typically, with a "qualified retirement plan," when you are fifty-nine and a half, you are eligible to start withdrawing from these plans "without penalty." That means Uncle Sam allows you to start collecting some of your own savings money. However, once you start to withdraw money from these plans, *you are hit with taxes on that money.*

Once again, let's return to the seed and the harvest. Naturally you would like to get tax breaks on the price of your seed money (the contribution and accumulation stages) in the spring, and also on the harvest (the distribution stage). Later, we will show you how to reap your harvest tax-free.

The Roth Alternative—Still Too Many Strings

There is one savings alternative approved by Uncle Sam that works better for most people. It's called the Roth IRA or Roth 401(k), named for Senator William V. Roth Jr. of Delaware, who championed the legislation for it.

The Roth IRA or 401(k) allows you to sock away already-taxed dollars in a savings or retirement plan. You do not pay taxes on it when you start to withdraw that money. But you cannot withdraw the interest you earn without penalty until you are fifty-nine and a half years old.

There are other strings attached to the Roth IRA or 401(k). If you make more than a certain amount of money, you cannot make contributions to a Roth IRA. What's more, you cannot withdraw money from a Roth (without incurring taxes and a penalty) until at least five years after the first contribution is made. After five years, you are able to access your basis (the money you invested in it) without tax or penalty. One good thing about a Roth is that you are not required to withdraw a minimum amount from a Roth IRA at age seventy and a half, as you are under a traditional IRA.

You are years away from the age at which you can take money out of these qualified savings plans without paying possible penalties and tax. Wouldn't it be nice to put money in a nonqualified savings plan, without any IRS penalties, so you can use the money when you need it? In chapter 8, we'll go into detail on these often confusing retirement plan options. For now, we simply want you to understand that you don't have to follow the crowd that invests in qualified savings plans, only to see Uncle Sam pick their pockets when they are finally old enough to reap the rewards.

Please keep your mind open to the possibility that there may be smarter alternative advice about IRAs and 401(k)s than you might have heard about from more traditional CPAs, investment advisors, or company benefits specialists.

Even if you have already started on some of these plans, you are young enough to make an early course correction. Stick with us, and we'll show you how smooth the sailing toward financial independence can be.

AUTHORS' NOTE

After reading this chapter, you should now have a basic understanding of income tax brackets. In an effort to keep illustrations simple and conservative throughout the remainder of this book, we will use a 20 percent marginal tax bracket in most examples and a 25 percent bracket in a couple of examples. A 15 percent federal tax was the rate for incomes between $16,051 and $65,150 for a married couple filing a joint tax return or between $8,026 and $32,550 for a single taxpayer in the tax year 2008. The federal tax rate was 25 percent for incomes between $65,151 and $131,450 for a married couple filing a joint tax return or between $32,551 and $78,850 for a single taxpayer in 2008. Most states (41 out of 50) also have a state income tax rate that ranges from 2.5 percent to 9.3 percent; so we are assuming an average of 5 percent for most taxpayers. Therefore, a 15 percent federal income tax rate plus a 5 percent state income tax rate equals a combined marginal tax bracket of 20 percent.

REMEMBER THIS

- Three common mistakes that taxpayers make are: (1) losing the use of thousands of dollars by withholding too much from their paychecks; (2) filing a short income tax form rather than itemizing deductions on the long form; and (3) assuming that deferring taxes on qualified retirement savings will save you taxes.

- You can often find money to sock away in savings by redirecting some of the unnecessary tax withheld in your paycheck, which can compound and grow to a sizable sum over time.

- The marvel of compounding will allow your money to grow exponentially over time. Using the Rule of 72 you can estimate how many years it will take to double your money at a given interest rate.

- The longer you wait to begin saving and investing, the more you will need to set aside to achieve your goals.

- File a long-form tax return to take advantage of itemized deductions if you own a house—not the EZ form.

- You can leverage otherwise payable income tax to help you accumulate more savings and investment dollars for your retirement, rather than giving Uncle Sam unnecessary income tax during the contribution, accumulation, or distribution years.

- To get the biggest bang for your retirement bucks, it is crucial to have retirement savings that are tax-free when you make contributions, tax-free when your savings are accumulating, and tax-free when you take distributions from them.

- Knowledge is power. By redirecting just $4,000 a year of otherwise payable income tax through mortgage interest deductions, a person can accumulate more than $1 million over a forty-year period in a conservative side fund that earns an average of 7.5–8 percent interest compounded annually.

LEARNING LINKS

Visit www.MissedFortune.com/Millionaire-By-Thirty and click on the learning portal for chapter 5 to:

- Use a simple calculator to help you determine how many exemptions you could claim on your W-4.
- Download a free, complimentary current-tax-year Federal Tax Rate Schedule for single, married (filing jointly or separately), or head-of-household taxpayers that also contains other valuable information such as personal exemption amounts.
- Download a free copy of the current state individual income tax rates for all fifty states.

CHAPTER 6

From Renter to Homeowner in One Leap

Buy Your Primary Home *Now* Rather Than Rent

MANY YOUNG PEOPLE ASSUME that they should rent before they own. Why? Because that's what everyone does when they're starting out, right? We'd like to challenge that thinking. And in fact, we'd like to outline not only *why*, but also *how* home ownership is possible sooner rather than later.

> *Aaron:* You're making a decent living now, Christopher. Have you thought about buying your first home?
>
> *Christopher:* I don't like to think about it. The idea of buying a home is scary! Besides, I'm sure I don't have nearly enough saved for a down payment.

Thinking about buying a first home can make anyone nervous. And it is a big enough step that you should never make a snap decision. But contrary to popular opinion, putting off buying a first home until you save enough money for the down payment is unnecessary.

Imagine for a moment that you are taking a fistful of hundred-dollar bills (the ones with Benjamin Franklin), stuffing them in a canister (like the one you might keep sugar in), and burying the canister in a hidden spot somewhere. Ten years from now, you could dig it up, and although you won't have earned any interest on that money, you've got real money to spend.

Now imagine that you took that same canister and tossed it in a river. You watched as it floated downstream, wondering what lucky person—if anyone—might retrieve it. In ten years, you could search in vain for that canister. That money is gone. Imagine if you did that on the first day of every month for the next few years. Distressing, isn't it?

If you currently pay rent on your home or apartment rather than owning it, tossing it away is exactly what you're doing with your money! There is no way to recoup that spending. You get no frequent-flyer miles. You get nothing beyond your shelter.

At least if you had buried the money in the backyard, you would be able to access it. Granted that fistful of bills would be worth less than it is now due to inflation, but you'd have *something* to show for it.

Now consider this: What if you took that same fistful of money and invested it in a home? Especially if you borrowed the money (in other words, if you obtained a mortgage), it is likely you could get all the money you invested out of it later. It is also likely that this home will increase in value over the next several years. In that case, the house would be worth 30, 50, or even 100 percent more when you sold it, thanks to appreciation.

You really can make this investment *right now*. It is an investment we believe in and one we think is more secure than any stocks, bonds, or mutual funds over time. There's something else, too—unlike your mutual fund or 401(k), at least you can sleep in this investment!

We would like to convince you that you *can* buy your own home, even if you are just beginning your time in the workforce, or even if you are still in college. There are traditional and nontraditional ways you can purchase a home soon, without waiting months or years to save enough for a large down payment. And by envisioning it as an investment, we hope you'll reach a new comfort level with owning your own home.

As we mentioned earlier, there are three things you can do with money: spend it; lend it; and own with it. Renting is spending. Owning is the real deal, the ticket to your future financial freedom.

A few years ago, a *Wall Street Journal* article noted that "buying a first home can be a scary twenty-something experience. Between the Realtors, lenders and mortgage brokers, it's hard to know where to start and whom to trust. Plus, buying demands two resources often in short supply at this age: money, and the ability to commit— not to a person, but to a place."[*]

We want this to be a positive, exciting experience for you, rather than a scary one.

Let's dispel a myth about money—follow our directions and you will be using other people's money to buy the home. As for the ability to commit, you are not buying something you are going to keep forever. Yes, you are making a commitment to a place, but nobody says you must stay there for a certain length of time. Your parents or grandparents may have looked upon buying a home as a thirty-year proposition—that's why there are thirty-year mortgages. But things are quite different today; the current generation is much more mobile than the Boomer generation.

Here's another false idea: Twenty-somethings don't own; they rent. The truth is, the percentage of homebuyers under age twenty-five is growing. As of 2006, U.S. Census Bureau data indicated that 25 per-

---

[*] Jennifer Saranow, "Home Buying Can Be a Scary 20–Something Experience," *Wall Street Journal Online*, Aug. 24, 2004.

cent of those under twenty-five currently own their own home—
that's one in every four.*

How are they accomplishing this?

Exchange Your Rent for Home Ownership

As we have explained, the amount you pay in rent is not deductible on your tax return. If you are in a 20 percent tax bracket, an
interest-only mortgage payment can be 25 percent greater than the
rent you might be paying, without increasing your after-tax outlay.
For example, a person paying $800 in monthly rent could prob-
ably afford to make a $1,000 monthly house payment (25 percent,
or $200, more). This is true because the homeowner gets to write
off that $1,000 of deductible mortgage interest. In a 20 percent tax
bracket, that means the homeowner will receive $200 back—in
other words, pay $200 less in tax—making the net after-tax house
payment really only $800. Of course, a homeowner needs to also
pay for property taxes and homeowner's insurance—so that should
be taken into consideration when on a tight budget.

FIGURE **6.1**

EXCHANGE YOUR RENT FOR HOME OWNERSHIP 7 Percent Interest Mortgage with Monthly Rent Equivalent			
MONTHLY RENT	15-YEAR MORTGAGE	30-YEAR MORTGAGE	INTEREST-ONLY MORTGAGE
$550	$76,488	$103,336	$117,857
$650	$90,395	$122,125	$139,286
$750	$104,302	$140,913	$160,714
$850	$118,209	$159,702	$182,143
$950	$132,116	$178,490	$203,571
$1,050	$146,023	$197,279	$225,000
$1,150	$159,930	$216,067	$246,429
$1,250	$173,837	$234,856	$267,857

Assuming a 20% Marginal Tax Bracket

---

* "Demography is Destiny: Realtors Meet the Future of Real Estate," press release,
National Association of Realtors, May 18, 2007.

Please refer to figure 6.1. In the first column are various monthly rent amounts. The second column lists the amount of money a homebuyer could borrow using a 7 percent interest, fifteen-year mortgage equaling the same monthly outlay as the monthly rent in the first column. The third column lists the amount of money a homebuyer could borrow using a 7 percent, thirty-year mortgage equaling the same monthly outlay as the monthly rent in the first column. And the fourth column lists the amount of money a homebuyer could borrow using 7 percent interest-only mortgage with the same monthly outlay as the monthly rent in the first column. We will discuss these various mortgage options later in this chapter.

Of course, qualifying for a mortgage is contingent on the homebuyer being able to qualify for the mortgage from an income and creditworthiness standpoint. As already explained, better mortgage interest rates are offered to those borrowers who have higher credit scores. Also, most mortgage lenders will not approve a mortgage loan if the applicant's proposed mortgage payment (including tax and insurance) added on top of all other monthly debt payments exceeds 40 percent of monthly gross income.

Three Traditional Ways for First-Timers to Finance a Home

You may already be familiar with the traditional ways for first-time buyers to finance a home:

- FHA loans
- VA loans
- Conventional mortgages

For decades, millions of first-time homebuyers who do not have a large amount of money stashed away for a down payment have gone to the Federal Housing Administration (FHA) or Veterans Administration (VA) for help with mortgages. It is one of the most common methods of reaching ownership status without coughing up a big down payment.

FHA loans are mortgages that you can get while putting as little as 3 percent down on the financing of a single-family house. They are available from traditional lenders but are insured by the federal Department of Housing and Urban Development. You must meet certain basic credit qualifications, and your loan requires mortgage insurance that is added to the cost of the mortgage (to protect the lender against loss should a borrower default and foreclosure become necessary). An FHA loan may also require various inspections and reports that other lenders do not.

Although the government limits how big your FHA-insured mortgage can be, the ceiling can be surprisingly generous. The basic ceiling as of May 2007 was $200,160, but was much higher in certain expensive counties and states—over $362,000 as of May 2007 in high-priced parts of the continental United States, and over $544,000 in Hawaii and Alaska.

The Veterans Administration offers *VA-guarantee loans* with *no down payment* on a primary residence. You can only get a VA loan from a conventional lender if you are a veteran who meets certain qualifications and conditions, of course. The VA charges a funding fee instead of mortgage insurance.

Both FHA and VA loans can be a good deal for you *even if you have cash for a down payment* because we believe you should put as little of your own money into the down payment as possible.

For your parents' generation, the typical way to buy a house or condo was to obtain a *conventional mortgage*—a loan from a bank, credit union, or mortgage company that holds the first lien on the property. Usually, lenders require buyers to make a 20 percent down payment. *Satisfying the down payment with your own cash is the least desirable method for financing your first home purchase* because there are excellent alternatives that allow you to become an owner without waiting to have that much cash.

Three Ways to Buy When You Don't Have Cash for the Down Payment

If you do not have enough for a large down payment and the closing costs yourself, you can still become a homeowner. There are three excellent ways to "satisfy the down," which means finding the money to cover the down payment:

- Borrow the down payment from the seller.
- Borrow the down payment from a relative.
- Satisfy a down payment through a second mortgage.

You can join the growing ranks of young homeowners, even if you think you might want to move in a year. Buying a home is probably the most expensive thing you will ever do, but it is easier now thanks to the Internet, and it can be done over and over again. If you need to relocate in a year, or simply pay less for a mortgage, you can either refinance or sell it and buy a different home. (You can buy your *second* home more quickly than you might think. We'll get to that in the next chapter.)

Emron: How Harmony and I Bought Our First Home

Two weeks after my twenty-third birthday, my wife, Harmony, and I bought our first home in a Utah suburb. We had used the Internet extensively to look for properties. Every Saturday and Sunday, we drove around to actually see the different homes. By the time we found one we liked, we were well-acquainted with all the homes and prices in the area.

I did not have any credit history at the time. But my dad had taught me there were ways that even without a credit history or thousands of dollars in the bank, we could purchase a house.

I don't want anyone to think we used some questionable "no money down" scheme. Instead, we chose a For Sale by Owner, or FSBO, home. If you look hard enough and regard your first house as your starter home, you can find a house to buy with unconventional financing, often using the sellers themselves.

When a buyer buys a home directly from the seller, and the buyer makes monthly payments to that seller rather than to a mortgage company, this is called "buying on contract." The buyer and seller draw up a contract with the seller acting as the lender. Thus the seller is "carrying the contract."

The first time I proposed this to a couple selling their home, I was turned down. They were more comfortable doing the traditional kind of sale. So Harmony and I found a different home for sale by owners who were willing to listen to my nontraditional idea.

In a casual conversation, I learned that these sellers didn't need the money from the sale of their house to put toward the purchase of their next home—they already had bought it. Instead, they were allocating the money from their current house to pay for their children's future college education. They planned to put it in a bank savings account paying a measly 1 percent. So I asked them, "How would you like to earn 7 percent on that money instead?"

"Of course we'd like 7 percent, but where in the world can we find a rate like that?"

"You'll get that from me," I replied.

I explained that we could draw up a contract in which they would take the place of a mortgage lender. Each month I would pay them the equivalent of a mortgage payment that included 7 percent interest. Even though the fixed mortgage rate at the time was closer to 5 percent, I was happy to pay the extra 2 percent in order to buy rather than rent a home.

This way, I didn't have to cough up one dime in a down payment, and it was a win-win scenario. A competing buyer offered them only $168,000, but these sellers saw how my payments on $170,000 would allow them to sock away money for their kids' college education—and get a much better interest rate than any bank would pay at the time.

So Harmony and I moved in, and for one year we paid the sellers about $1,000 a month. That was a little bit more than we were paying in rent, but because we were paying a mortgage, we could deduct the interest on our tax return. That saved us around $200 each month, so we did not have to take money from one of the monthly "envelopes" in Quicken earmarked for expenses such as entertainment, car payments, and so forth.

During that first year, we paid an amount not much greater than what we were paying in rent, and we were thrilled to be owners, not renters. Meanwhile, the previous owners got 7 percent interest from us that they would not otherwise have received.

Borrowing from the Seller to Make Your Down Payment

At the time Emron bought his first house, conventional mortgages were being offered for as little as 5 percent. It's logical to ask if he was upset that he was paying a higher rate. The answer: No!

Would you rather have a single apple or twenty apples at the end of the year? By paying a little bit higher rate, he took a chance that he would be able to make twenty times his money—by owning a home that would appreciate and that he could refinance at a cheaper interest rate after one year. It was much better than waiting around for a year, struggling to save enough for a down payment.

Back in chapter 3, we talked about three kinds of people: those who *pay* interest, those who *earn* interest, and those who pay interest to earn *more* interest. Emron was on his way to becoming the third kind of person.

You can be this kind of successful borrower as well. Don't be afraid of a first mortgage that's higher than normal. In Emron's case, after one year his house was worth 10 percent more than $170,000. In real estate terms, it had appreciated 10 percent. The lesson here is, if you are willing to pay a little bit more, you can eventually make money, rather than throw it away on rent.

After one year, Emron and Harmony's starter house—which, on paper, they had bought for $170,000—was appraised for

$187,000. Also, they now had a credit history, so they were able to get a cheaper mortgage (through a conventional mortgage lender). They weren't required to pay off the contract that soon, but they chose to do so because the house had appreciated enough to obtain a first and second mortgage sufficient enough to pay off the contract with the sellers. They used most of the money from the new mortgage to pay off the former owner. The previous owners "won," because Emron was paying them 7 percent on their equity that they had earmarked as their college savings account during that year, earning a higher interest rate than they would have with their money in the bank.

Three years later, the house had appreciated even more—to over $240,000. Look at what they accomplished: They had, on paper, made $70,000, simply by moving forward immediately to buy a home, rather than putting off a purchase until they had saved up a down payment.

Lease with an Option to Buy

Another way you can get into your first house is by finding or creating the opportunity to *lease with an option to buy* by simply discussing this option with any seller. This method is similar to the way Emron and Harmony bought their first house. Typically you pay a small nonrefundable deposit (which will go toward your down payment if you decide to purchase later on) and you can lock in a purchase price for the house. Some sellers who are offering a lease option may have you pay an extra $100 or $200 a month, which can also go toward a future down payment on top of the deposit you made. Understand that while you are leasing the home, your lease payments are not tax-deductible. You can write up the length of the lease for whatever period is best for you and the seller. During the term of the lease (usually one or two years), you can exercise the option to purchase the home for the price you previously agreed on or you can move. However, if you decide to move, the owner keeps your deposit and the extra payments you may have been making. On the other hand, if the house appreciates in value while you are leasing, you can receive all that appreciation if you end up exercising your option and purchasing the house.

Borrowing from a Relative

What if you are not able to find a seller who will finance your down payment and mortgage, even for just one year? The second solution is to find a relative—your parents, an uncle, or someone like that—who will become your lender. Once again, it's a win-win deal.

You approach your relatives by making it a business proposition: Here's a chance to earn 7 percent (or two percentage points higher than whatever the going rate on savings is in your town) on their money, with a house as collateral.

Or suggest it as a partnership—if they give you 10 percent of the purchase price for the down payment, they make a good profit: 10 percent of the value of the house when you ultimately sell it (which, due to appreciation, is likely to be worth much more).

In either case, it is an attractive investment. You draw up a contract so they don't have to trust only your word—they also have your signature. You secure the loan with a trust deed note that says you are borrowing the money for this home.[*]

If you agree to pay a rate that results in a monthly payment higher than your rent, and it makes your cash flow difficult, where could you find the mortgage money? In your paycheck! You simply

---

[*] When a relative is providing money for a down payment, lending guidelines may dictate that your relative be a cosigner on the loan. Or the lender may require that your relative "gift" you the money to be used for the down payment rather than "lend" it to you. Later when you sell the home or refinance it, you could gift the same amount back although you're not legally required to do so. *Under current tax law, annual gifts of $12,000 can be given by an individual to another without a gift tax.* Check with a professional mortgage planner for proper ways to involve a relative.

go to your employer and raise the number of exemptions on your taxes, so less is deducted each pay period. When it's time to pay Uncle Sam taxes at the end of the year, you get a great deduction in mortgage interest.

> **LINK TIP:** Go to www.MissedFortune.com/Millionaire-By-Thirty, and under the learning portal for chapter 6 you can find samples of such arrangements, templates for leases, rent agreements, and so forth, as well as detailed information on interest-only and negative amortization loans.

Roommates Can Finance Your House, Too

Buying your first home takes some creativity, but as Emron points out, "You are also forcing yourself to learn something; your financial maturity grows. You learn financial discipline. If I had not bought my home, I would never have received that real-life education."

Another way to buy your first home even when you don't have much income is to rent extra space to a roommate or two, whose rent money each month you can use to pay the mortgage. They get a good place to stay, while you get the tax benefits of owning, thanks to Uncle Sam.

Your mortgage interest is deductible, as we have shown. You are also earning passive income in the rent you collect, but this income is often more than offset by the expenses you incur, such as mortgage interest, depreciation, and repairs. It is pretty simple for a tax preparer to calculate all this on your income tax return.

> **LINK TIP:** To see a sample of a Schedule E tax form showing how rent appears as passive income, and depreciation and maintenance appear as deductions, go to www.MissedFortune. com/Millionaire-By-Thirty under the learning portal for chap-

ter 6. You can also find a typical rental agreement that you can download and use with your roommates.

Yet another possibility: Buy a house using a roommate as a partner. Naturally you want to be careful in choosing dependable partners. Even if that person is a friend, you must treat this as a business. Do your due diligence by checking your potential partner's credit. If their credit history is poor, they may be financially immature, and you might prefer to have them as renters.

Why would a roommate want to buy rather than rent? For the same reason that you do: to keep from tossing money in the river month after month. You may have to educate your potential roommates on the value of the deal to them in terms of appreciation and tax breaks. If they are still not comfortable, you can revert to the "I own and you rent from me" scenario.

Satisfying the Down Payment Through a Second Mortgage

If neither of the former options works for you, it is possible to get part or all of the down payment from the mortgage lender.

Here's an example. Our daughter Mindy and her husband Brian recently moved to Iowa City for four years while Brian attends dental school. They found a town home in a neighboring community for $140,000.

They got what's called an 80/10 mortgage: 80 percent is a first mortgage at 6.75 percent, which covers most of the purchase price; 10 percent is the second mortgage at a higher rate that goes toward satisfying half of the 20 percent down payment.

They then borrowed the remainder of the down payment—10 percent—from Aaron. Also, the seller agreed to pay $2,000 of the closing costs just for the asking.

With luck (and based on historical figures), four years from now they should be able to sell the town home for $175,000, assuming a conservative rate of appreciation—5.5 percent a year. At that time, instead of paying Aaron back $14,000, they pay him $17,500, or 10 percent of the home's value.

It is another win-win. They have a house; Aaron makes extra money; and they have enjoyed a four-year partnership. Can anyone guarantee that? No. But if history is a guide, the market for starter town homes in a college town like Iowa City is a safer investment than the stock market.

What happens if four years from now the market in Iowa City is soft? Traditionally, prices go down mainly on expensive homes. Rarely do prices turn negative on starter homes, which cost less and exist in a more conservative marketplace. What's more, there is almost always demand for starter homes in a college town. Brian and Mindy won't necessarily see 20 or 30 percent appreciation, but all anyone expects from a starter home is 3 to 7 percent appreciation per year.

Mindy and Brian researched the area before purchasing their town home and found that almost identical town homes within a stone's throw away had sold four years before for $108,000 and now were selling for $140,000—a 5.5 percent appreciation rate.

The important point is that Mindy and Brian's combined first and second mortgage payments total $735 per month, which is only $588 after the tax benefits. Most three-bedroom apartments in Iowa City rent for considerably more than that.

Starting with a Starter Home

Your first home may not be as spacious as your "dream home" or located in your dream neighborhood. But you can usually get a decent starter home that is nicer than the place you rent, costs no more each month than a rental home, and helps you learn the basics of real estate. Because you are just starting out, you may have to be willing to compromise on all of your wishes.

There are some locations in the United States where real estate prices are very expensive, such as Manhattan, San Francisco, or Boston. The price of an extremely modest studio apartment in New York City can run as much as $500,000. In such a case, it may be necessary to go into a partnership with your parents or other relative or even a roommate so that the combined income, resources, and credit will allow you to qualify for the required mortgage and down payment.

Remember that something like an FSBO house (or a condo), such as the one Emron and Harmony found, with owners who are willing to finance your purchase, benefits both the seller and you. Your seller saves money by doing all the work that typically is done by a real estate agent. That often means a lower sale price for you.

Why? When a house is listed with a real estate agent, the agent provides valuable professional services that can protect both the seller and the buyer. In return, the seller typically pays the agent a fee that can be as high as 6 percent. In Emron's case, this would have meant that the seller would have had to pay an immediate $10,200 to the agent at the closing.

The point here is that buying your first house is educational. Owning your own home can lead to opportunities for greater financial gain, as we'll explain later. And it might help to realize that while you're making a significant commitment, it is not a lifetime commitment. Enjoy the experience, and prepare yourself to optimize your upcoming equity.

Where Should You Go When You Need a Mortgage?

If you are able to satisfy the down payment through seller financing or through financing from a relative, but you still need to obtain a mortgage for the balance of the cost of the house, what do you do next? I'm sure you have heard about all kinds of mortgage providers, as well as different mortgages themselves. It is important to choose the provider and the mortgage that suits your savings style, your lifestyle, and your cash flow.

There are three main sources you can look to:

- A local bank or credit union
- A mortgage banker
- A mortgage broker

Your neighborhood *bank* or *credit union* is one choice. But it may not offer you the best rate or as many choices. Don't simply go to your bank and accept the first mortgage package a bank officer suggests. Although your parents might have financed their first home this way, there is a remarkable array of mortgages out there.

A *mortgage banker* is an individual or financial institution dedicated solely to property loans. This also includes primary lenders, some with nicknames like Freddie Mac, which are organizations that were created to purchase mortgages mainly from savings and loans companies. They in turn sell their loans to secondary lenders such as the publicly held Fannie Mae (the Federal National Mortgage Association) or other companies.

Alternatively, you might do well with a *mortgage broker*—a kind of wholesaler who represents more than one lender. Mortgage brokers help to arrange about 60 percent of all home loans. They may offer competitive rates because they do the shopping for you among primary lenders. Mortgage brokers are paid a fee for their services.

Compare rates and terms. Seek a mortgage that matches your ability to make monthly payments. Consider how long you expect to stay in the home; if it is just a few years, an ARM or deferred-interest loan, explained below, with a low initial rate might work best for you.

Ask a savvy financial services professional or mortgage specialist to show you a selection of mortgages that fit your needs. If this book was given or recommended to you by a financial professional, you may choose to seek his or her services, as well as advice from your personal tax advisor.

If you are not acquainted with a professional trained in the strategies contained in this book, don't despair. There are thousands of professionals nationwide who have completed our training programs.

LINK TIP: To locate a properly trained professional from among our national network of financial experts, visit www.Missed Fortune.com/MissedFortuneAssociates.

What Kind of Mortgage Should You Get?

Here is how to sort out the difference between a fixed-rate or an adjustable-rate mortgage, a fifteen-year or a thirty-year mortgage, an interest-only or a negative amortization mortgage.

Fixed-Rate Mortgages

Fixed-rate mortgages are the "plain vanilla" of mortgages. The most common are designed to be paid off in a fifteen- or thirty-year period.

With long-term fixed-rate mortgages, the interest rate you pay never changes, nor does the amount of each payment. They are usually amortized (paid off through regular payments that reduce both the principal amount of the loan and the interest on it). These payments do not change unless late-payment interest and/or penalties are incurred.

You may come across the acronym PITI, which stands for principal, interest, taxes, and insurance. To make sure taxes and home insurance are always current, a lender may require regular payment for those and have them held "in escrow," that is, by a third party. The tax and insurance portion of the monthly fixed-rate mortgage may vary each year depending on those rates, but the sum of the principal and interest is constant.

Adjustable-Rate Mortgages

Adjustable-rate mortgages, sometimes called ARMs, are loans in which the interest rate may vary over the life of the loan. A lender may accept a lower qualifying income on an ARM because of initially lower interest rates. This makes housing more affordable, but in exchange there may be a provision for interest rates to escalate in the future. To determine the amount of such adjustments, interest rates in ARMs are tied to one of many indices that represent the general movement of interest rates, such as the prime rate (the rate banks charge their most creditworthy commercial customers). Lenders may also add percentage points, referred to as the "margin," to the index to determine the adjustable rate.

ARMs are available for a mortgage term ranging from ten to forty years. Typically, there is an interest rate cap that limits how high the interest rate can go. The periodic rate cap limits the adjustments during a stated time period. Even though the interest rate can go up, the increase in the monthly payment amount may be limited by the loan's payment cap.

You may be offered a conversion option, which allows an ARM to be converted to a fixed-rate mortgage without the normal expenses of refinancing. To exercise this option, the lender usually charges a certain number of percentage points, and the borrower must exercise this option during a specific time period.

Interest-Only and Deferred-Interest Mortgages

The *interest-only mortgage*, usually offered as an ARM, has become very popular, especially for those people who want a low monthly payment. In general, we like an interest-only mortgage or option ARM that allows you to pay interest only or defer a portion of the interest, because the amount paid will fit into almost any budget. At the same time, you can usually deduct the interest each year to reduce your taxable income.

A *deferred-interest mortgage* is sometimes referred to as a "negative amortization" loan because you are not paying down the principal.

Thus your overall mortgage obligation grows, rather than declines, each year. It is useful for those who would rather allocate future dollars (which are cheaper) to cover a mortgage than use today's more expensive dollars. In other words, you trade some of your future cash flow to avoid a negative cash flow (by applying money to the principal that earns nothing) at the beginning.

Some financial advisors criticize interest-only and option ARM loans because they say the low rates lure people into buying a more expensive house than they can realistically afford and subject them to higher monthly payments once they reach the point where they must begin paying off the principal.

We recommend that you should *only buy a house that you could afford assuming you were required to make a thirty-year or fifteen-year amortized mortgage payment*. But instead, you take out an interest-only or deferred-interest loan and then set aside the difference between the two payments in a liquid, compounding side fund. As noted, this takes a lot of self-discipline.

During the second half of 2007, America began to experience what is referred to as "the mortgage meltdown." A lot of houses were foreclosed on by mortgage lenders when interest on option ARM mortgages adjusted to higher rates: Those borrowers had no liquidity or could barely afford their initial monthly house payment and subsequently got behind on their mortgage. Most foreclosures occurred with borrowers who had low credit scores and had no liquid money in savings. Loans made to such borrowers are referred to as "sub-prime." Because of this, many lenders tightened their belt and discontinued many lending programs for sub-prime borrowers, making it harder for homebuyers to obtain a mortgage unless they met higher guidelines. (Some mortgage lenders even went out of business due to the meltdown.) If homebuyers follow the advice in the Missed Fortune series, they should have the liquid cash available to handle most emergencies—or be able to afford higher payments if interest rates increase in the future. As you are about to learn, it's a lot better to have access to liquid cash and not need it, than to need money and not be able to get it—especially if it's tied up in your house.

As you will see in the next chapter, we usually refinance fairly often to harvest lazy, idle dollars that accumulate in the house due to appreciation. So we don't ever worry about a loan converting to an amortized loan, because chances are, we have already refinanced before that happens. The bottom line is, you are best off when you do *not* pay down principal, thereby lowering your acquisition indebtedness and losing the tax benefits. To learn more about the rules that the IRS has established that dictate the limitations regarding how much mortgage interest a taxpayer can deduct, please refer to my other works, *Missed Fortune 101*, *Missed Fortune*, and *The Last Chance Millionaire*.

You should shop around to find an interest-only loan or option ARM that comfortably fits your financial situation. A word of caution: You must be *extremely disciplined* and have a system of accountability to use deferred-interest (negative amortization) loans. Otherwise, you may end up consuming your equity or buying more house than you can comfortably afford. It is imperative that you set aside the money you are saving (by not paying even the interest accruing each month) to make more money.

For young adults just getting into their first home, an interest-only mortgage or an option ARM is the most aggressive choice that you could make. If you have a system where you borrow to conserve, not to consume (you'll hear that phrase a lot from us!), a thirty-year amortized mortgage works *well*, an interest-only mortgage can perform *better*, and an option ARM with deferred interest can perform *best*.

Figure 6.2 shows a grid comparison of different mortgage options using a $200,000 mortgage as an example. It is easy to interpolate from this chart based on any mortgage amount you might be considering. For example, if you were considering a $100,000 mortgage, all of the numbers on the chart would be half of the amounts shown. If you were considering a $150,000 mortgage,

FIGURE 6.2

COMPARISON OF DIFFERENT MORTGAGE OPTIONS ON A $200,000 MORTGAGE

DIFFERENCE IN PAYMENTS NET AFTER TAX ON A $200,000 MORTGAGE AT 7.25% INTEREST (2.5% START RATE ON DEFERRED INTEREST MORTGAGE)

	15-YEAR MORTGAGE	30-YEAR MORTGAGE	INTEREST-ONLY MORTGAGE	DEFERRED INTEREST MORTGAGE
15-Year Mortgage	-	$464.50	$621.58	$1,042.51
30-Year Mortgage	$464.50	-	$157.08	$578.00
Interest-Only Mortgage	$621.58	$157.08	-	$420.93
Deferred Interest Mortgage	$1,042.51	$578.00	$420.93	-

SETTING ASIDE DIFFERENCE IN PAYMENTS INTO SIDE FUND EARNING 8 PERCENT INTEREST YEAR 1 ENDING BALANCE

	15-YEAR MORTGAGE	30-YEAR MORTGAGE	INTEREST-ONLY MORTGAGE	DEFERRED INTEREST MORTGAGE
15-Year Mortgage	-	$5,821.57	$7,790.21	$13,065.65
30-Year Mortgage	$5,821.57	-	$1,968.64	$7,244.08
Interest-Only Mortgage	$7,790.21	$1,968.64	-	$5,275.44
Deferred Interest Mortgage	$13,065.65	$7,244.08	$5,275.44	-

SETTING ASIDE DIFFERENCE IN PAYMENTS INTO SIDE FUND EARNING 8 PERCENT INTEREST YEAR 15 ENDING BALANCE

	15-YEAR MORTGAGE	30-YEAR MORTGAGE	INTEREST-ONLY MORTGAGE	DEFERRED INTEREST MORTGAGE
15-Year Mortgage	-	$180,581.92	$241,647.99	$404,212.83
30-Year Mortgage	$180,581.92	-	$61,066.08	$223,630.92
Interest-Only Mortgage	$241,647.99	$61,066.08	-	$162,564.84
Deferred Interest Mortgage	$404,212.83	$223,630.92	$162,564.84	-

CORRESPONDING MORTGAGE BALANCE AT THE END OF YEAR 15

	15-YEAR MORTGAGE	30-YEAR MORTGAGE	INTEREST-ONLY MORTGAGE	DEFERRED INTEREST MORTGAGE
MORTGAGE BALANCES	-	$149,459.48	$200,000.00	$304,678.64

Assuming a 20% Marginal Tax Bracket

all of the numbers would be 75 percent of the numbers shown. Likewise, a $300,000 mortgage would be 50 percent more than the numbers shown.

Figure 6.2 contains four sections. The top section shows the difference in monthly payments after tax on a $200,000 mortgage at 7.25 percent interest between a fifteen-year mortgage, a thirty-year mortgage, an interest-only mortgage, and a deferred-interest mortgage. To maintain liquidity and accumulate enough money to "pay off" your mortgage sooner than by paying off the mortgage company, the second section of the chart shows how much you would have if you set aside the difference in payments between the various mortgages into a side fund earning 8 percent after one year. The third section shows the balance of liquid cash you would have if you set aside the difference in payments between the various mortgages into a side fund earning 8 percent over a fifteen-year period. The bottom section shows you the amount you would still owe on the different mortgage options at the end of fifteen years. By studying the third and fourth sections, you will see that if you use a deferred-interest mortgage rather than a fifteen-year amortized mortgage and save the difference in payments, you would have about $100,000 more if you used your side fund to pay off your mortgage ($404,212 minus $304,678). Likewise, if you chose a deferred-interest mortgage rather than a thirty-year amortized mortgage and saved the difference in payments, you would owe a net of about $80,000 ($304,678 minus $223,630) at the end of year fifteen on your deferred-interest mortgage compared to owing $149,459 on your thirty-year amortized mortgage.

Borrow to Conserve, Not to Consume

Why are we so insistent about buying a home as a crucial step toward financial freedom? Because you are really not putting money into the house—you are obtaining a mortgage, which is among the safest investments in this country! When you satisfy the down payment by borrowing from the owner or a relative, all you are doing is bypassing the middleman.

When you get a mortgage from the middleman, it is a bank, credit union, or mortgage company. Why is this lender willing to lend you money for your house? Because that company is doing what every lender does—borrowing money at one rate and lending or investing it to earn a higher rate.

FIGURE 6.3

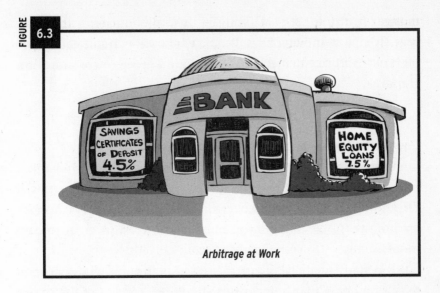

Arbitrage at Work

Who is the lender borrowing from? It might be you. If the lender is a bank or a credit union, it is "borrowing" from its depositors. It is thrilled to have you deposit money with them in a savings or checking account. Why?

Because they know they can borrow your money and pay you 3 percent, 4 percent, or 5 percent interest, and then reinvest or loan that money to earn 6, 7, 8, or 9 percent interest. They make a profitable difference, or spread, and they literally make millions.

Wouldn't you like to make money the same way? The technique of buying and selling investments to take advantage of small differences in price is called *arbitrage*. As an individual, you can achieve great results by doing your own arbitrage. It starts with borrowing to buy your first home.

But first, you need to commit one concept to memory: Borrow to conserve, not to consume.

Earlier, we mentioned that your "second mortgage" might be in the form of a home equity line of credit, or HELOC. Unfortunately, too many people treat this kind of loan as a credit card. That's a bad idea. You can see home equity lines of credit darting all over the lakes in the summertime in the form of boats and personal watercraft. In the wintertime, you see them gliding across the snow in the shape of snowmobiles. People who borrow home equity and then use it to buy depreciating assets are buying to consume, not conserve.

Congratulations—You Are Becoming Your Own Banker!

In the next chapter, you will learn to become your own banker. In buying your first home, you will have taken a giant step in that direction. You will have discovered that you can use OPM. You are learning that, like a bank, you must pay interest in order to earn more interest. This is the road to becoming a Thriver.

Too many financial planners and self-help gurus who appear on television argue that homebuyers should try to pay off that mortgage as quickly as possible or even get a fifteen-year mortgage rather than a thirty-year one. This may be *good* advice for the Strivers. But there is *better* advice if you want to be an Arriver. And the *best* advice for those who desire to be Thrivers is to ignore their suggestions.

Why? Because, as we have suggested before, you are not going to stay in your starter home for a lifetime. There's a good chance you won't be there more than five years.

Also, you are probably not even going to keep the very first mortgage you get for more than a few years, because, as we will show in the next chapter, you don't want lazy, idle dollars to pile up as appreciation in your house. You want to put that money to work for you, which means refinancing often. That's the way to become a millionaire by your thirties.

Remember a while back where we talked about assets and liabilities, as well as preferred debt versus nonpreferred debt? Like a bank, you now have assets (your home) and liabilities (your mortgage, as well as any student loans and/or credit card debt). And like a bank, your greatest liability is also your greatest asset—the mortgage allowed you to own an appreciating asset, and the interest on that mortgage, as you have just seen, is tax-deductible.

Christopher: Okay, Aaron, I've gotten past the scary part, and I'm now about to close on my first home. But my uncle's financial planner says a mortgage is like an eight-hundred-pound gorilla in the room. He says that as soon as we can, we should be making extra principal payments on it.

Aaron: Every time you make an extra payment, you are saying to your lender, "Here's some extra dough. Don't bother to pay me interest on it." Sounds silly, doesn't it? What's more, you will be killing your partner, Uncle Sam. The more you reduce your mortgage, the less the amount of interest you have to claim as a tax deduction.

Christopher: But I just got a raise! I've got more ready cash! I can get out from under the mortgage in half the time.

A raise is great. But a mortgage is great, too. *It's your friend, not an eight-hundred-pound gorilla.* You should always take that extra cash and put it in a conservative side fund, where you can earn interest on it. You will sock away so much money that in just a few years you'll have accumulated enough to pay off your mortgage entirely, *if you wanted to.* You would have enough money to pay off your mortgage sooner than sending your raise to the mortgage company. That should help you relax. Meanwhile, you have continued to get your mortgage-interest tax break from Uncle Sam.

LINK TIP: To see how much quicker you can have your home paid for by saving your extra mortgage payment in a side fund or by saving the difference between a fifteen-year or thirty-year mortgage versus an interest-only or deferred-interest mortgage, go to www.MissedFortune.com/Millionaire-By-Thirty and click on the learning portal for chapter 6.

Help! My Equity Is Trapped Inside My House!

Let's imagine for a moment that like Christopher, you have finally found your starter home. You have arranged some kind of financing. But you're still worried about that mortgage.

Once you understand how useful a mortgage can be, you will realize why Emron, Aaron, and I are always talking about "lazy, idle dollars." And you'll see why we are not fond of the idea of "building up equity" in your house through mortgage prepayments.

The truth is, even if it took us many months longer to accumulate enough money to cover what we owe on a mortgage, we would still prefer to keep that mortgage rather than pay it off. Why? *Because that's the way to maintain liquidity and safety of principal.* Back in chapter 3, you learned about the LSRR test for serious cash: liquidity, safety, and rate of return.

Once you pay off your mortgage, your money is neither liquid nor safe. Sounds like a paradox, doesn't it? Before we move on to the heart of equity management, it's time for a homebuyers' quiz.

Emron: Don't you want to be able to access your money, Christopher, rather than giving up control to the mortgage company?

Christopher: Well, sure.

Aaron: Wouldn't you like to reallocate extra mortgage payments to earn you extra money, rather than just lie there in a lender's bank?

Christopher: Of course I would.

Emron: Do you know how much money you would earn if you put the biggest down payment possible on a house—that is, if you paid cash for it?

Christopher: No.

Aaron: I hate to disillusion you, but the answer is, nothing! All that money and not a dime in interest!

Christopher: Wow! If that's the case, I need help! My equity is trapped inside my house! What do I do now?

I hope you get the drift. "Building up equity" is a phrase from your parents' generation. All it means is that you are allowing lazy, idle dollars to stay trapped inside that nice new home you've bought. Let us assure you that help is at hand. Turn the page. In the next chapter we explain the secret to liquidity, safety, and rate of return, and show you how to manage your home equity to propel you toward financial independence.

REMEMBER THIS

- You can buy your first house sooner than you may think, often resulting in a monthly payment that is no more than you are paying in rent.
- You can satisfy a required down payment on the purchase of a home using little or none of your own cash by borrowing the down payment from the seller, a relative, or through a second mortgage.
- You can buy your first house with little or no cash down by using traditional financing through an FHA or VA loan or through creative methods such as a lease with an option to buy.
- Consider using a professional mortgage planner to help you find the most appropriate mortgage for your particular set of circumstances.
- Accumulate the extra money that you would be paying on an amortized mortgage versus an interest-only or deferred-interest mortgage in a conservative side fund to increase the liquidity, safety, and rate of return of your home equity. You will accumulate enough money to cover your mortgage balance sooner than by sending extra principal payments against the mortgage.
- Buying your first home will be one of the most significant steps toward achieving financial independence.

LEARNING LINKS

Visit www.MissedFortune.com/Millionaire-by-Thirty and click on the learning portal for chapter 6 to:
- Listen to an audio summary of chapter 13 of *Missed Fortune*, entitled "Pay No Money Down—Alleviate Cash Down Payments When Purchasing Real Estate"

- Listen to an educational audio recording to learn how to manage home equity successfully to create wealth.
- View historical real estate appreciation rates by state from 1940 up through recent years.
- Find samples of seller financing, templates for lease and rental agreements, as well as information on interest-only and deferred-interest (negative amortization) loans.
- Find a sample of a Schedule E for a tax return showing how rent appears as passive income and depreciation and maintenance appear as deductions.
- Download a typical rental agreement to use with your roommates.
- Locate a properly trained professional from among our national network of financial experts in asset optimization and equity management.
- See how much quicker you can have your home paid for by saving your extra mortgage payment in a side fund or by saving the difference between a fifteen- or thirty-year amortized mortgage payment versus an interest-only or deferred-interest mortgage payment.

CHAPTER 7

Real Estate Equals Real Wealth

Develop Real Estate Equity and Manage It Successfully

AS YOU KNOW BY NOW, BUYING A HOME is one of the first big steps toward wealth optimization. But you're probably curious about what comes next. Here's where we start to lay out the other steps that will lead you to a more abundant life by your thirties.

Emron: Nicole, how do you and Christopher feel now that you've taken the plunge, bought a house, and have moved in?

Nicole: It's great! My parents can't believe we've done it. We're set for life now, right?

Emron: You're set for now, but I bet you'll be ready for a getaway or even a vacation in Hawaii before long.

Nicole: Sounds great, but honestly I don't think we can afford a big vacation. Hotels are expensive.

Emron: Who needs a hotel when you can buy your own vacation home or condo?! And then, like Aaron, you can build or buy a third home to use as an investment. It's all part of the plan to become millionaires by your thirties.

Let's go back to that fistful of Ben Franklins in chapter 6. And let's play house with you and your spouse standing in for Christopher and Nicole. Each month, you pay your mortgage. It's hardly more than you were paying for rent. You are no longer tossing a tin can full of money in the river. You are sending money each month to your mortgage lender.

You've made a good start. However, if you do nothing more than watch your house appreciate, you might just as well bury your money in your backyard. It is locked in your house. We're about to show you how to rescue it and make it work as hard as you do.

Successful equity management means removing lazy, idle dollars when they begin to become locked in your house as equity, and then investing that money to maximize liquidity, safety, and rate of return. In other words, it's about doing what banks and credit unions do to amass a tremendous amount of wealth.

You're about to learn our strategy of turning your very first home into an asset that can help generate the money for the vacation home you've always wanted, and, beyond that, creating an extra $1 million or more in resources for you.

You'll recall that in advanced budgeting, you list your assets on one side of a ledger and your liabilities on the other. As long as your assets exceed your liabilities, you are in good financial health, particularly if those assets are liquid.

Our strategy puts enough money in your right-hand pocket (the asset pocket) to be able to wash out the mortgage liability that's in your left-hand pocket—so that your house is paid for on your balance sheet in a shorter time frame than through traditional methods. You then enter a financial comfort zone in which you can double your net worth on those assets every seven to ten years.

Most people view a mortgage and mortgage interest as negatives. As you have already learned, mortgage interest can be a big

When you have real estate assets in one pocket and the equity repositioned to the other pocket, you have more assets working for you.

positive, because every dollar you pay reduces your tax liability at the end of the year. *But you can turn your first mortgage from merely a tax aid into a remarkable generator of income.*

Separate Equity from Your House

Let's imagine that you have bought a house with a fair market value of $200,000 and you have a mortgage (or mortgages) totaling $200,000. Every month you send money to your mortgage lender. Meanwhile your home is appreciating in value at, say, 6 percent. After one year you will have paid $15,000 to your mortgage lender if your net mortgage payment is interest-only at 7.5 percent, but Uncle Sam will give you about $3,000 of that back, thanks to tax-deductible interest. Your home will be worth $212,000, and you still owe $200,000, giving you an equity of $12,000.

In your very first year you retained all $12,000, from your home appreciating, which is the same amount you paid in net mortgage interest ($15,000 minus $3,000 in tax savings) that would have otherwise gone down the river in rent! Supposing instead that the house went up in value 10 percent that year and the mortgage interest was at 6 percent, you would have $20,000 of equity accumulated (10 percent growth on $200,000) with a net mortgage cost of about $9,600 (6 percent interest on $200,000 is $12,000 minus 20 percent in tax savings [$2,400] equals $9,600). You not only retained all $9,600 that you paid in net mortgage interest, but you also realized an additional $10,400 due to the house appreciating 10 percent—for a total of $20,000. How many of you would like to have an additional raise of $10,000 to $20,000 each year?

The first step in our strategy is to protect and preserve as much of your home equity as possible—in the first case $12,000—by separating it from your house so you can invest it for the highest liquidity, safety, and rate of return. In addition you have saved $3,000 in tax.

You'll recall that in chapter 3 we spoke about the three lodging places for money: houses of bricks (low-risk, conservative investments), houses of sticks (moderate-risk investments), and houses of straw (higher-risk investments).

In a strictly financial sense, your home is not a house of bricks; it is a house of sticks. Real estate is a moderately risky investment. With a lot of equity locked inside, your house (and thus your money) may be vulnerable to:

- Gusts of wind—the ups and downs of the real estate market cycle, or, literally, tornadoes, hurricanes, etc.
- The big bad wolf—layoffs or economic upheavals

If that wind howls or the big bad wolf starts beating on your door, wouldn't you rather keep your equity in a house of bricks?

On the other hand, a house of bricks—a conservative investment—is one that offers you the highest return with the greatest amount of safety, the lowest amount of risk. When smart investors are offered a new investment, they ask three questions:

1) "Can I get my money back when I want it back? Is it
    liquid?"
2) "Is it guaranteed or insured? How safe is it?"
3) "What rate of return can I get?"

Liquidity, safety, and rate of return—LSRR, or what we call
"LASER"—are the three key elements of a prudent investment. A
house is where your family should reside, not your money. So the
trick is to take your equity from your house of sticks (your house)
and lodge it in a house of bricks (a safe, smart investment).

To help illustrate this point, let's imagine your financial consul-
tant comes to you with an investment for your consideration.

Financial planner: Here's an account where you determine
the amount and length of time for monthly contributions to
continue. Is that okay?

You: Sure.

Financial planner: You can pay *more* than the minimum monthly
contribution if you like, but not less. If you attempt to pay less,
the financial institution keeps all of the previous contributions!
Is that still okay?

You: Hmmm. Not happy about that.

Financial planner: The money you are investing is not safe from
loss of principal. In fact, each contribution made to the account
results in *less* safety. Also, the money in the account is not
liquid. The return? Well, it earns a zero percent rate of return.

You: This sounds very unattractive.

Financial planner: With each contribution to this investment,
your tax liability increases. And when the plan is fully funded
there is no income paid out.

You: Thumbs-down.

This obviously does not meet the "LASER" test of a prudent investment. Yet you probably recognize that you may already have such an account or may be considering one. That's right! *It's a house with a traditional amortized mortgage.*

Let's take another look at the canister in your backyard. Is it liquid? Yes, as long as you can remember where you buried it, right? Is it safe? Yes, as long as your dog doesn't know where you buried it. Is it earning a rate of return? No. In fact, it is probably losing value with even a nominal amount of inflation.

What is the difference between the money in the tin can in your backyard and the hundreds or thousands of dollars that we tie up in the bricks, mortar, wood, and cement in the foundations of our houses? There is no difference, except that the money buried in your yard is probably more liquid and safe than the dollars tied up in a house.

"But wait!" you say. "Isn't this the house you just urged us to buy in the previous chapter?"

Yes it is—but buying it was only the first step. You still need to turn your house into an investment that is *liquid*, *safe*, and has a good *rate of return*.

The "LASER" Test: Liquidity, Safety, Rate of Return

How important is *liquidity*? Remember, the gusts of wind howling outside your house represent not just ups and downs of the real estate market, but the gyrations of the stock market, the literal winds of natural disasters, and also the unexpected expenses of life (a car repair, unemployment, marriage, a new baby, etc.). So if something goes sour, you want to be able to access your money. You do not want to be exposed to external forces over which you have no control.

If you had a house that flooded in Louisiana in 2005, wouldn't you want to be in a position—with one phone call or electronic fund transfer—to access $50,000, $100,000, or $150,000 of cash so you could start to rebuild your life? But if that house was paid off, your money would be trapped inside those flooded rooms. You can see why we sleep better at night with our home equity removed and in a position of liquidity, rather than trapped in the property. And you should too!

Why do we put such emphasis on the *safety* of principal? Because we believe that with serious cash, your credo should be similar to that of a physician: "First, do no harm." With your principal safe, whether your house goes up in value or down, you don't lose. You are not at the mercy of the real estate market, banks, or a mortgage company. Again, you sleep better at night.

It may seem as though throughout your short adult life, the real estate market has stayed strong. Yet over the past twenty years, nearly every real estate locale has gone soft at times. We know people with modest homes in Newport Beach, California, and Naples, Florida, whose homes have skyrocketed in value. Modest homes purchased for $125,000 less than twenty years ago are now worth $1 million because they doubled in value about every six years. But these Californians and Floridians expressed concern about a real estate bubble. If or when bubbles burst, those house values could temporarily plunge by 20 to 30 percent.

If they leave the equity in those homes and the homes go down in value, those folks can lose hundreds of thousands of dollars. Lenders foreclose *first* on houses containing the *most* equity.

Here's what happens. There's a low balance remaining on the mortgage, so the lender has a chance of getting the rest of the money owed by turning the house over to a foreclosure sales specialist. If there's a high mortgage balance (because you've removed the equity), the lender won't be as quick to foreclose; the loan balance could now be more than the foreclosure price.

We show people—and we want to show you—how to separate equity when your home appreciates, so that if your house loses value temporarily, you will *not* lose. Our strategy teaches you to maintain safety of principal no matter what home values do.

What about a soft real estate market, when there are more homes for sale than there is demand to buy them? You are likely to sell your house more quickly and for a higher price if you have a high mortgage balance. Why? You can be flexible, and you can carry the contract or lease the house with an option to buy if it doesn't sell right away. You don't have to wait until someone cashes you out.

Understanding Equity

Here's another question to consider: How do you calculate the *rate of return* on your home equity?

That's easy. It is zero.

"Whoa!" you say. "You've told us a house would be our best investment!"

It is—*as long as you separate the equity from the house and put it someplace where it earns money.*

Owning a house *is* a good investment, but the *equity* in your home is not a prudent investment on its own—it earns nothing when it stays trapped inside your house. When you paid a down payment on your house, how much interest is the mortgage company paying you on that down payment? Nothing. No interest. No dividends. Zip.

It doesn't matter whether you are in Iowa City or New Orleans, or even New Jersey, where some houses have been averaging 12 percent a year appreciation for the last thirty years. Appreciation makes the house more valuable, not the equity you have accumulated in it. The rate of return on home equity is always the same. Zero.

Instead, your equity *costs* you money.

What cost do you incur on your home equity? Many people think the answer is nothing. Not true! You have given up the opportunity to earn a rate of return.

Some people think that when they pay down their mortgage, they are getting a rate of return on the house.

Not so! Equity *grows* on paper as a function of the house appreciating and the debt reducing, but equity still has no rate of return! When we separate it from the house and position it in a side fund or other investment, we give it the ability to earn a rate of return.

"Whoa!" you shout. "When I get a mortgage loan, that sure costs me money—I've got to pay interest!"

True! When you separate the equity from your house, by getting a mortgage in the first place or refinancing later, you still incur a cost. That's the interest you pay in order to separate the equity from your house. But when you invest that money at a *higher rate* than you are paying in mortgage interest, you are exploiting the spread—or practicing arbitrage.

That's exactly why banks and credit unions are so willing to give you a mortgage in the first place—they pay you interest on your savings accounts in order to take your money and loan it back or invest it at a higher rate to make more interest. This is how you become your own banker. By paying the cost of a mortgage in order to make a greater return, you are behaving exactly like a smart banker.

Truth is, you're going to do even better than you think. Your cost—the mortgage interest—is tax-deductible. So rather than paying, say, 7 percent, you are actually paying only about 5.5 percent once you factor in the tax savings.

Later in this chapter we have scenarios that show you just *how to earn up to $1 million* in the next ten to seventeen years by borrowing your home equity at one rate and growing it in liquid, safe investments that earn a higher rate. That's the secret of equity management.

LINK TIP: Go to www.MissedFortune.com/Millionaire-By-Thirty to use Emron and Aaron's Wealth Scenario Generator. By inserting some basic data in it, we will guide you on what price house you can afford with different types of mortgages, and how you might separate equity from the house and invest it in a side fund.

Free Up Those Lazy, Idle Dollars

Let's say you remove equity from your house and put it into a safe side fund or some other prudent investment. Instead of sitting inside your house, lazy and idle, those dollars are now earning money. If your mortgage is costing you 7.5 percent in interest and this investment earns the same rate, 7.5 percent, *you still make money*. Why? Because your mortgage payments are calculated at simple interest and are tax-deductible, whereas the investment is growing via tax-favored compound interest.

As we've mentioned before, the small spread between what the money costs you and what it earns is called arbitrage. That sounds esoteric, but that is exactly what banks do when they collect money from you and pay you one rate on your savings, and then charge a higher rate when they lend the money to someone else.

Equity management is really being able to optimize one of your greatest assets—to take the extra dollars stuck in your house and turn them into homemade money. Managing equity properly empowers you with the ability to generate a substantially increased net worth. We will point you to what we regard as the best, most prudent investments in chapters 8 and 9. Meanwhile, we simply want you to absorb the idea that once you own your first home, you have an asset that you can use to invest for a bright future.

Let's use a really simple example of this strategy in action.

Look at figure 7.2, and imagine that the empty paper cup represents Aaron's house before he has put a nickel in it, and the sports-drink bottle represents his bank account, with $100,000 in it.

For simplicity's sake, we'll assume the house is worth $100,000. Thus, on his balance sheet when filling out his financial statement, Aaron lists the house as an asset. Even though technically it is "empty," like the cup, on paper it counts as an asset because that's the house's value. Aaron's cash account (the bottle could represent a savings account, certificate of deposit, or insurance policy) with $100,000 of liquid cash in it is also an asset. So his total assets amount to $200,000.

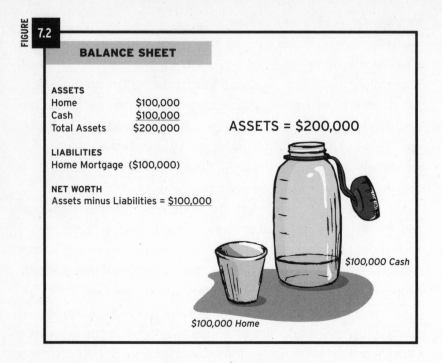

FIGURE 7.2

BALANCE SHEET

ASSETS
Home $100,000
Cash $100,000
Total Assets $200,000

LIABILITIES
Home Mortgage ($100,000)

NET WORTH
Assets minus Liabilities = $100,000

ASSETS = $200,000

$100,000 Cash

$100,000 Home

Now suppose that although Aaron has $200,000 of assets, he has also taken out a $100,000 mortgage on his house. That's a liability, so his net worth equals $100,000 on day one (assets $200,000 minus liability $100,000 equals net worth $100,000).

But from day two forward, Aaron can increase his net worth if he keeps the two assets separated. Let's assume he takes 20 percent of his cash and pours it into his house—he makes a down payment, or pays down that percentage of his mortgage.

What if Aaron paid cash for his house, or paid it off? What, then, did Aaron just do to his assets? He took one $100,000 asset (his cash) and another $100,000 asset (his house) and combined them together into one $100,000 asset. He has just *cut his assets in half*.

On the other hand, what happens if he separates 100 percent of equity from his house and pours it into a bank account or investment? He *doubles* his assets.

FIGURE 7.3

What happens when we pour all of our cash into our property?

$0 Cash

$100,000 Home

We cut our assets in half...
$100,000 IN ASSETS

Now assume that his house appreciates 5 percent this year. At the end of the year his house—that "empty" cup—is worth $105,000. He has made $5,000 because of appreciation. If Aaron paid off his mortgage—and thus filled the cup—what would it be worth? The same: $105,000.

Why? Because *equity has no rate of return*. People tend to think that because they are "reducing" their debt or their house is appreciating, the equity in their house has a rate of return. Not so! Equity *grows* as a function of the house appreciating and the debt reducing, but equity has no rate of return! When we separate equity from the house and reposition it in the bottle, we give it the ability to earn a rate of return.

FIGURE 7.4

What happens when we separate equity from our property?

$100,000 Cash

$100,000 Home

We double our assets...
$200,000 IN ASSETS

Let's assume that Aaron's separated equity that is now in a prudent investment—the liquid in the bottle—earns 10 percent this year. What is this worth at the end of the year? A cool $110,000. So he has made $10,000. His house appreciated $5,000, so he has made a total of $15,000. That's triple what he made when his house was paid off!

Of course, we are overlooking something. Aaron has mortgaged his house, and so he is paying interest—the cost for the use of that money. But just as banks and credit unions borrow at one rate and put their money to work at a higher rate, Aaron's still ahead of the game provided his separated equity is making a higher rate of return than the mortgage is costing him.

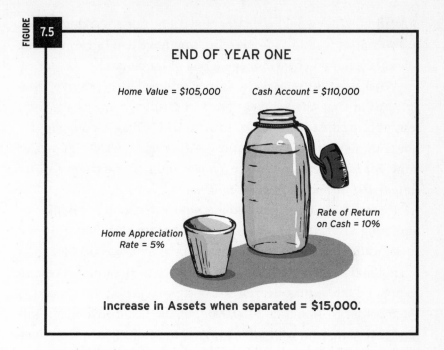

FIGURE 7.5

END OF YEAR ONE

Home Value = $105,000   Cash Account = $110,000

Home Appreciation
Rate = 5%

Rate of Return
on Cash = 10%

Increase in Assets when separated = $15,000.

LINK TIP: Go to www.MissedFortune.com/Millionaire-By-Thirty and click on the learning portal for chapter 7 to see how you take equity out of a house with a mortgage and invest it to generate wealth by borrowing at one rate and investing at the same or different rate.

If Aaron was paying 7.5 percent interest on the $100,000 mortgage, it would cost him $7,500 a year. But he made a total of $15,000 by separating his equity so his net profit is $7,500 ($15,000 minus $7,500 equals $7,500). But is it really costing Aaron $7,500? It isn't if the interest is deductible on his tax return. In a 20 percent tax bracket the $7,500 is really only costing him $6,000 (20 percent less), because Uncle Sam will be giving him back $1,500 in otherwise payable tax. Can you see why Aaron would gladly pay $6,000 (net interest expense) to earn a total of $15,000 for a net gain of $9,000? If he didn't do this, he would only realize the $5,000 of house appreciation. What would you rather have, one horse working for you or two horses working for you? Can you have two horses working for you even if you owe money on one of the horses?

What this illustrates is the marvel of drag—safe, positive leverage. Just as that kite we mentioned in chapter 3 must have some resistance against it to climb, so Aaron uses drag—leveraging his house by separating equity from it—in order to watch his wealth grow. For more detail on equity management, please refer to *Missed Fortune 101* or *The Last Chance Millionaire*.

Figure 7.6 illustrates how a homeowner can stack up $1 million by separating $100,000 of home equity just one time (by borrowing the equity using a mortgage) and paying 7.5 percent tax-deductible simple interest and putting those lazy, idle dollars to work earning 8 percent compound interest tax-free. Over a thirty-year period the net cost of the mortgage(s) would be $180,000, but the liquid investment side fund that started out with $100,000 grew to $1,006,266. After deducting the $100,000 mortgage, the net growth over thirty years would be $906,266. Later in this chapter, we'll show you how you can achieve similar results—a million dollars accumulated in a side fund—in just ten years, and you don't have to start out with $100,000 of equity.

As we've explained the concept of equity management, it might sound pretty straightforward to those of you who have completed the required math courses in elementary and high school. Yet a few years ago, I met with three finance professors at a university who told me they all taught their students why they should take out fifteen-year amortized mortgages rather than thirty-year amortized mortgages.

"Oh, really. Tell me why you do that," I said.

They basically said, "Duh . . ." (or maybe they said "Doug," and I misheard them). "If you just bite the bullet and pay a little higher mortgage payment for fifteen years, you'll save yourself from paying lots of interest, and you'll have your house paid off in a shorter time frame. After that, you can start saving."

I asked if they had ever taken a differential between a fifteen-year

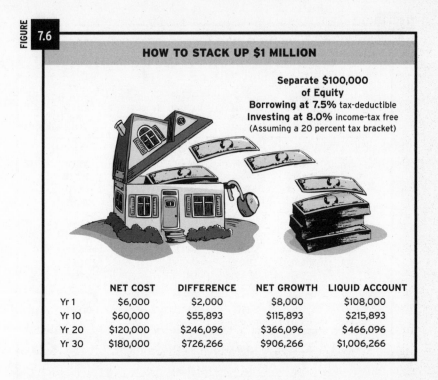

FIGURE 7.6

HOW TO STACK UP $1 MILLION

Separate $100,000
of Equity
Borrowing at 7.5% tax-deductible
Investing at 8.0% income-tax free
(Assuming a 20 percent tax bracket)

	NET COST	DIFFERENCE	NET GROWTH	LIQUID ACCOUNT
Yr 1	$6,000	$2,000	$8,000	$108,000
Yr 10	$60,000	$55,893	$115,893	$215,893
Yr 20	$120,000	$246,096	$366,096	$466,096
Yr 30	$180,000	$726,266	$906,266	$1,006,266

amortized mortgage payment and a thirty-year amortized mortgage payment and set aside that difference *including the tax savings* during the first fifteen years of a thirty-year mortgage. They had not.

I crunched some numbers on a calculator for them, and the results astonished them! On a $100,000 mortgage, in thirteen and a half years, there was enough money in a conservative side fund to totally pay off the thirty-year mortgage—eighteen months sooner—using some of Uncle Sam's money instead of the homeowner's. That example was using a 34 percent marginal tax bracket. Even if you are in a 20 percent tax bracket you can accumulate enough cash in a side fund to pay off a thirty-year mortgage in fourteen years, maintaining much greater liquidity as shown in figure 7.7.

The takeaway lesson here is: Don't accept what a finance professor tells you unless he or she can show you the math. They often have only considered traditional, conventional concepts.

FIGURE 7.7

ACCUMULATING THE NET DIFFERENCE BETWEEN A $200,000 30-YEAR 8% MORTGAGE PAYMENT AND A 15-YEAR 8% MORTGAGE PAYMENT IN A SIDE FUND EARNING 8% INTEREST**

END OF YEAR	[1] 30-YEAR MORTGAGE LOAN BALANCE	[2] 15-YEAR MORTGAGE NET PAYMENT AFTER TAX	[3] 30-YEAR MORTGAGE NET PAYMENT AFTER TAX	[4] DIFFERENCE BETWEEN NET PAYMENT AFTER TAX	[5] DIFFERENCE EARNING 8% COMPOUNDING
1	$198,329	$19,788	$14,422	$5,365	$5,794
2	$196,520	$19,907	$14,450	$5,457	$12,151
3	$194,560	$20,036	$14,480	$5,556	$19,124
4	$192,438	$20,177	$14,513	$5,664	$26,771
5	$190,140	$20,328	$14,548	$5,780	$35,155
6	$187,651	$20,493	$14,586	$5,906	$44,347
7	$184,955	$20,671	$14,627	$6,043	$54,421
8	$182,035	$20,863	$14,672	$6,191	$65,461
9	$178,873	$21,072	$14,721	$6,351	$77,557
10	$175,449	$21,298	$14,773	$6,525	$90,809
11	$171,741	$21,543	$14,830	$6,713	$105,323
12	$167,725	$21,808	$14,892	$6,916	$121,219
13	$163,375	$22,095	$14,958	$7,137	$138,624
14	$158,664	$22,406	$15,030	$7,376	$157,680 *
15	$153,563	$22,743	$15,109	$7,634	$178,539 ◄

$24,976.61

EXCESS CASH BEYOND MORTGAGE BALANCE

* Notice that you would have enough money in your liquid side fund to pay off the mortgage sometime just after the 14th year.
** Both the 30-year mortgage and the 15-year mortgage are amortized assuming 8 percent interest, and a 20 percent marginal tax bracket.

Whatever else you do, when you separate your equity from your house, you boost your assets. Even though there is a cost—the simple interest you pay on a mortgage—it makes sense to take out a mortgage and use it to grow your assets. In this example, we are talking about paying 7.5 percent *simple, tax-deductible* interest on a mortgage in order to make 7.5 percent *compounding, tax-favored* interest on an investment. You don't make millions overnight, but you make a profit in the first year, more in the second, and still more in the next eight years.

One last point: If Aaron were to follow conventional, same-old, same-old financial advice, the prudent investment—the bottle of liquid cash—would not amount to as much as we've shown because he would have to pay tax on his earnings.

But what if that investment were free of tax? Remember the second marvel? It's thrust—tax-free accumulation. Finding an investment that is tax-free provides a thrust that multiplies your assets year after year so you can soar by the time you are in your thirties. We'll introduce you to such investments in chapters 8 and 9.

LINK TIP: Return to www.MissedFortune.com/Millionaire-By-Thirty, Emron and Aaron's Wealth Scenario Generator, to review how to use the magic of compound interest, tax-free accumulation, and safe, positive leverage with various mortgages to generate as much as $1 million or more in assets, starting with that first home you have just bought.

Repeat After Us: "Refinance, Refinance, Refinance"

We have tried to explain in the most digestible way the basics of equity management. But we haven't finished. By using the appreciation in your house to establish its value, *you can refinance your mortgage as often as every two to three years*, and thus reap the benefit of additional dollars that are accumulating in that bottle. In this way, your house becomes a money machine—provided that when you refinance, you use the money to conserve, not to consume. With each refinanced loan, you have more and more dollars to sock away in prudent investments.

Remember how we described Arrivers and Thrivers? The Arrivers have learned the basic principles of wealth accumulation; they have learned financial discipline and they understand the three marvels of compound interest, tax-free accumulation, and safe, positive leverage.

Arrivers become Thrivers by taking these simple concepts of wealth accumulation and repeating them over and over again. Within the next ten to fifteen years, by (1) refinancing your home as it appreciates, (2) separating the equity, and (3) investing the profits in liquid, safe, prudent investments with a good rate of return, you can have your money earning more than you do by the time you are in your thirties.

These strategies can truly work. In real life, Aaron bought his first house several years ago at the age of twenty-three for $205,000. Rather than throw his money away on rent, he turned the same money into mortgage payments.

Two years later, it was worth $315,000. After just two years, he had, on paper, an extra $110,000 in equity. He was then in a position to go to a lender and refinance. He could remove a cool hundred grand that he did not have before, which he invested in a smart, safe investment—an indexed universal life insurance policy that credited as high as 15 percent interest during that year. We'll talk about the amazing results you can get from maximum-funded life insurance in chapter 9.

An Alternative to Frequent Refinancing—but Only for the Disciplined

If refinancing every few years does not sound appealing to you, there is an alternative: deferred-interest loans. But we share this with a big word of caution. *This option is only for the extremely financially disciplined.*

As we explained in the last chapter, deferred-interest loans (what some refer to as negative amortization mortgages) are structured so that while you pay only a portion of the interest, the actual grand total of the loan grows larger as the years go by.

In effect, such a mortgage keeps the equity from accumulating as rapidly in the house, allowing you to accumulate it elsewhere. So you don't need to go back to a mortgage lender as often. Because of this, holders of such mortgages may not need to refinance as often as every two or three years, thereby saving money on closing costs and other charges.

However, we must warn you that before you sign on the dotted line for a deferred-interest loan, you *must* have a system for conserving and investing money along the way. If you spend the money that you are not paying in interest, you are wading into deep water.

This is not the kind of loan for anyone who is what we call a financial jellyfish, or even inexperienced young adults. It can be awfully tempting to spend the difference, or buy more home than you can afford. Unless you are confident that you will be able to set aside the money you save when you don't pay even all the interest owed each month (so that the money in one pocket *always* can cover the liabilities in the other), we recommend that you do not undertake a deferred-interest loan. An interest-only loan would be the better choice.

LINK TIP: Go to the section of the Wealth Scenario Generator found at www.MissedFortune.com/Millionaire-By-Thirty to help determine how you can use a deferred-interest loan properly or what type of mortgage can provide you the greatest liquidity, safety, and rate of return to accelerate your wealth.

Why Wait? Buy Your Vacation Home Now

Within a year or two of buying your first home, there's another investment that we believe can improve your quality of life and add even more wealth to your bottom line. What is it? Your second home—that cabin in the mountains, the condo by the lake, or perhaps a deeded timeshare in a relaxing location where you'd like to spend your vacations.

How can you afford it? The same way you were able to afford your primary home. By using the same strategy we described in chapter 6, you obtain a tax-deductible loan to cover the purchase price of your second home. (Once you have your first house and have established a credit history, it can be easier to qualify for a mortgage.) Remember, at the end of each year, the interest you have paid on it lowers your taxable income on your federal return.

By using our equity management system of investing the separated equity prudently, you can start enjoying a vacation getaway now, rather than waiting years and years.

Why is this such an ideal option for you? Mortgage interest generally is deductible on *both first and second homes*. In other words, Uncle Sam will help you pay for your vacation getaway.

And guess what? Your second home doesn't have to be a house. The tax code says a secondary residence can be a:

- Part-time city dwelling
- Condo
- Town home
- Cabin
- Boat
- Yacht
- RV
- Timeshare
- Fractional deeded property

(Sorry, Harley lovers; a sidecar does not count. A vehicle qualifies as a second home *only* if it has sleeping, cooking, and toilet facilities!)

Recall for a moment the sports-drink bottle and the paper cup. You can have the use of a second cup, separate the equity from it, and put some of it in a prudent investment—and at the same time profit from the appreciation that many second homes have enjoyed in the past few years, all while you retain the use of the money in a second bottle.

There's still another remarkable element involved in a vacation property. Your second home (or boat, RV, or timeshare) *can do double duty as a retirement plan*.

That's right! The cabin you enjoy next summer by the shore or

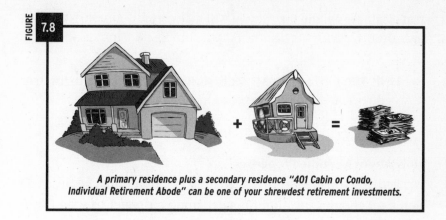

A primary residence plus a secondary residence "401 Cabin or Condo, Individual Retirement Abode" can be one of your shrewdest retirement investments.

in the mountains is a fine way to save money for your later years. It is our version of an IRA—an Individual Retirement Abode. Why sock away money in traditional IRA investments, when all the fun you get out of them is reading an annual financial statement? Wouldn't it be more fun to enjoy the same tax and appreciation benefits as an IRA but at the same time get away for recreation and build wonderful memories with your family and friends?

Even if you have already invested in a 401(k) at work and you have extra cash each month to cover a loan payment, a second home is an ideal way to optimize your wealth for a carefree lifestyle in the future. Make sure that you invest in an asset that will appreciate (go up in value) rather than depreciate (go down in value).

In chapter 10 of *The Last Chance Millionaire*, I explain how to establish an "Individual Retirement Abode (IRA)"—what I often refer to as a "401 Cabin" or "401 Condo." The chapter contains detailed examples of how to invest in your second home and retirement savings at the same time. (While I use terms like "401 Cabin" to describe the subject, there is not a reference in Section 401 of the Internal Revenue Code to this strategy.) In one example, I illustrate how a cabin or condo appreciating at 7.2 percent a year (thereby doubling in value every ten years) can be a better investment than the same money invested in an IRA or 401(k) earning as much as 10 or 11 percent because of the greater tax advantages you enjoy on real estate versus the tax hit you will take on an IRA or 401(k) when you retire.

LINK TIP: Go to www.MissedFortune.com/401Cabin to listen to a concise description of this strategy.

How About Multiple Properties?

Perhaps you are not that keen on a vacation home because you don't get enough vacation time yet, and you prefer to spend your weekends playing basketball with your neighbors. In that case, you could buy a second home and rent it out. Some of the same principles apply to rental properties—especially safe, positive leverage and tax deductibility.

If you find you enjoy buying, building, and/or managing real estate, consider a rental property as an alternative to or in addition to a second home. Through creating and controlling home equity in three or more properties, refinancing as often as possible, and managing the equity in excess of your mortgage balance over a period of years, you can be on the turbo track to financial independence even before your thirties. *The tax advantage of buying rental property is that you get to: (1) deduct the mortgage interest, (2) deduct maintenance and repairs, and (3) take depreciation on the actual structure.* Those three deductions are usually more than the income you receive in rent. It becomes a great tax benefit, saving you thousands of dollars in taxes. For more details, see the sections of my book *Missed Fortune* on "Liquidating Investment Real Estate Income Properties," in chapter 12, and "Focus on the Positive," in chapter 20.

LINK TIP: Go to www.MissedFortune.com/Millionaire-By-Thirty and click on the learning portal for chapter 7 for samples of how you might manage your equity in multiple properties, including rental real estate.

If you're Rick Hendrick or Jeff Gordon, would you rather have one NASCAR car to race or three?

Isn't Owning Multiple Properties a Lot of Work?

We suspect most of you are excited about taking control of your future. We hope you look forward to managing equity in your first home and doubling your pleasure and fun with a vacation home. But perhaps there are a few of you who are plagued by brain cramps with all this talk of equity, mortgages, refinancing, and investments.

It only takes a few hours a *year* to deal with refinancing and the other paperwork and research associated with managing equity. To make an extra $100,000 every two years as Aaron did, you may only have to spend about one hour a month. Isn't that worth it? Some young adults we know spend far more time than that to eke out an extra $500 with Mary Kay cosmetics sales or eBay trading.

Isn't it worth an extra hour or even ten hours each month to basically double your income?

Let us illustrate. *Here are three case studies . . .*

We have been discussing how to become wealthy utilizing the magic of: compound interest, tax-favored accumulation, and safe, positive leverage. A friend once taught me a ditty: "Good, better, best; never let it rest! Never let it rest, till good gets better and better gets best!" There are ways of taking advantage of these strategies as an Arriver, which is good—as a Thriver, which is better—or as a Super Thriver, which is best.

Figure 7.9 illustrates examples of three friends from college who all graduated with student loans of $20,000, and started making $50,000 a year in income. Barry, the oldest and the Arriver, reaches his first million in seventeen years. John, who is a bit younger than Barry and the first Thriver, reaches his first million in thirteen years. And Liz, the Super Thriver, reaches her first million in ten years, and she will probably be able to triple her million by the time the Arriver reaches his first million.

How did the Arriver do it? Barry, in the "good" example, first frees himself from throwing away money in rent every month and purchases a $215,000 home using a first and second mortgage averaging 7 percent interest. Instead of taking out a traditional thirty-year mortgage, he opts for interest-only mortgages, allowing him to save about $175 a month in his side fund.

Next he takes the new tax savings he is receiving from his new mortgage(s), and also adds in his tax savings from his student loan and invests that new money in his side fund. He does this by changing his exemptions at work, thereby decreasing his tax withholding by about $270 a month. He was also sending an extra $150 per month to pay off his student loan, but instead decides that that money would be better put to use by "paying himself first" in his side fund.

Prior to implementing this strategy, all Barry could afford to do was allocate 3 percent of his income ($103.87 after tax) to his side fund. Now by rearranging his affairs he is saving nearly 17 percent of his income! Barry understands that equity has no rate of return and his home is appreciating at an average of 7 percent each year. He refinances whenever he has more than $60,000 of equity (which is about every two to four years) and takes out the equity and starts a new side fund. Doing this repeatedly over the next seventeen years, he is able to add an additional $464,145 of lump-sum deposits to his side fund. By year six his net worth (home value plus side fund, minus liabilities and mortgage) is nearly $190,000. In another six years with the magic of compound interest, tax-favored accumulation, and safe, positive leverage, Barry's net worth has already accelerated to over $500,000. His net worth grows in excess of $1 million during the last five years.

How did the Thriver do? John, the Thriver, upon learning about Barry's strategy, decided to do the same thing but wanted to build upon it. Instead of renting, he bought a similar home nearby for the same price as Barry's home. He too took out an interest-only mortgage rather than a thirty-year amortized mortgage and saved the difference. He mirrored everything that Barry did; however, he realized that if it works with his personal home, why not try it out with a second real estate property?

So by the end of the second year John buys another home for $245,000 and begins renting it. He uses the rent and tax savings from his rental to cover the mortgage payments and any maintenance and repairs. He uses the same process of refinancing by taking the equity out of his rental home as often as is feasible—just like he is doing with his personal home. In thirteen years this allows him to deposit $281,743 on top of saving 17 percent of his income. After five short years, John has a net worth greater than $200,000—already more than Barry accumulated after six years. John reaches a net worth exceeding $500,000 in nine years and a net worth greater than $1 million in thirteen years—four years earlier than Barry.

How about the Super Thriver? After learning from both Barry and John, Liz really gets it and decides to fly past all of them. She also mirrors everything that Barry did. But instead of just buying one extra real estate property like John, Liz decides to buy an additional real estate property every two years during the next ten years. So, including her personal residence, she would own a total of five real estate properties. Just like John, Liz rents out her additional real estate, and uses the rent and tax savings to pay the mortgage(s) and maintenance and repairs. By refinancing her real estate every two to four years, Liz will be able to invest a total of $736,625 in addition to 17 percent of her income. This allows her to accumulate almost $2 million in real estate, and almost $1 million in her side fund. By subtracting her liabilities of $1,955,313 from her assets totaling $2,958,445, you'll see that she surpasses both Barry and John by reaching her $1 million net worth goal by the tenth year! If Liz continued on this path, she would have two to five times the assets or net worth as John or Barry would in the same time frame that they reach their first million.

FIGURE **7.9**

GOOD: MILLIONAIRE IN 17 YEARS

1 Instead of renting for $1,200 per month, purchase a home using a $215,000 mortgage.
2 Instead of taking out a 30-year amortized mortgage, take out an interest-only mortgage and **invest** the difference in your side fund.
3 Take the new tax savings from your mortgage and **invest** them in your side fund.
4 **Invest** the tax savings from your student loan interest in your side fund.
5 Invest the $150 per month extra you were applying to your student loan.
6 Invest 3% of your income in your side fund (or a company sponsored plan if you receive a match).
*7 Refinance with maximum cash-out six times (every 2-4 years) durning the following 17 years and invest loan proceeds in your side fund. (A total of $464,145)

YEAR 6		YEAR 12		YEAR 17	
Home Value:	$322,657.03	Home Value:	$484,221.19	Home Value:	$679,145.27
Side Fund: +	$148,950.70	Side Fund: +	$546,686.93	Side Fund: +	$1,070,223.17
Total Assets:	$471,607.73	Total Assets:	$1,030,908.12	Total Assets:	$1,749,368.44
Liabilities: -	$281,821.00	Liabilities:	$484,221.00	Liabilities: -	$679,145.00
Net Worth:	$189,786.73	Net Worth:	$546,687.12	Net Worth:	**$1,070,223.44**

BETTER: MILLIONAIRE IN 13 YEARS

1 Do the same with your first property as outlined in the "Good" Example
2 Purchase an additional piece of real estate within two years and refinance with maximum cash-out four times (every 2-4 years) over the following ten years and invest loan proceeds in your side fund. (a total of $251,651)

YEAR 5		YEAR 9		YEAR 13	
Real Estate:	$601,684.16	Real Estate:	$788,685.19	Real Estate:	$1,033,805.40
Side Fund: +	$184,861.13	Side Fund: +	$438,347.92	Side Fund: +	$933,745.11
Total Assets:	$786,545.29	Total Assets:	$1,227,033.12	Total Assets:	$1,967,550.51
Liabilities: -	$581,957.00	Liabilities: -	$712,922.00	Liabilities: -	$966,173.00
Net Worth:	$204,588.29	Net Worth:	$514,111.12	Net Worth:	**$1,001,377.51**

BEST: MILLIONAIRE IN 10 YEARS

1 Do the same with your first property as outlined in the "Good" Example
2 Purchase an additional property every two years (5 properties total) and refinance with maximum cash-out every 2-4 years over the following six years and invest the loan proceeds in your side fund. (a total of $580,405)

YEAR 4		YEAR 7		YEAR 10	
Real Estate:	$822,321.64	Real Estate:	$1,312,329.37	Real Estate:	$1,979,752.41
Side Fund: +	$111,930.60	Side Fund: +	$355,966.25	Side Fund: +	$978,693.49
Total Assets:	$934,252.24	Total Assets:	$1,668,295.63	Total Assets:	$2,958,445.90
Liabilities: -	$786,821.00	Liabilities: -	$1,248,890.00	Liabilities: -	$1,955,313.60
Net Worth:	$147,431.24	Net Worth:	$419,405.63	Net Worth:	**$1,003,132.30**

Assuming : A real estate appreciation rate of 7 percent.
Mortgage interest rates of 7 percent.
A side fund interest crediting rate of 8 percent.

So, no matter whether you just want to keep things real simple like Barry, or supercharge your wealth accumulation like John or Liz, you can be a millionaire in your thirties. But by all means, get in motion!

If you begin this process in your twenties and you want to become a millionaire by age thirty (or if you are in your late twenties or early thirties and you want to become a millionaire in *less* than ten years), instead of purchasing an additional real estate property every two years, increase the frequency to one new property acquisition per year or even one every six months. We have clients who have purchased as many as one or two per month. However, this can become overwhelming quickly if you are not careful. It can become a full-time endeavor requiring lots of attention. Focus on keeping it as simple as possible, developing a process and proceeding with care. Make sure that you are patient with your purchases of real estate, ensuring that payments on the property will not result in negative cash flow after applying the rent and tax savings. Always strive to maintain liquidity, safety of principal, and earn a rate of return by employing safe, positive leverage. Above all, have fun and enjoy watching your net worth soar into the millions!

Build Your Wealth with Equity Management

Earlier in this chapter, we showed how a house with equity trapped inside is not a prudent investment. Now that we've transformed it, it becomes a great investment.

Let's imagine that Aaron returns to Nicole and Christopher three years after they agreed to follow his suggestions.

Aaron: I'm really glad you refinanced your first house a year after you bought it, since it appreciated by 11 percent that year. You had paid $200,000 for it originally. One year later it was worth $222,000. So you got interest-only loans for $200,000. How did that work out?

Nicole: It worked out great! Our monthly mortgage payments were about $1,166 averaging 7 percent interest, tax-deductible. But we separated the additional $20,000 that we got from the refinancing, and we put that in a side fund that went up 9 percent that year.

Christopher: We were a little nervous about going beyond that, but watching how well others have done inspired us.

Nicole: So we found a small condo at the mountain resort we really like. It was priced at $160,000. Our credit history and our salaries were good enough for us to get an interest-only mortgage on that, too. And now we spend lots of weekends at the condo, and we rent it out much of the time we are not using it. It only costs us a net of about $300 a month.

Aaron: You've got two mortgages now. Are those payments difficult to meet?

Christopher: No! We use the $300 a month we already had budgeted for an IRA. Instead of putting it in an IRA, we use that money and the rental income we receive to pay the mortgage on the condo.

Nicole: Only in emergencies do we use the profits we are making in the side fund to help pay the mortgage on our primary home. Meanwhile, since the mortgage interest on both reduces our taxes, our bottom line is strong. We really don't feel strapped.

Christopher: Actually, we're amazed at how well it all works.

Aaron: Sounds to me like you're less stressed than you were when you were renting your first home.

Christopher: It's true. And it's not like we spend all our spare time on this. It only takes about an hour or so every month with the help of a property management company.

Aaron: So what's next?

Christopher: You're going to find this hard to believe, but we're about to refinance again. Our primary home has gone up a little more than 8 percent a year for the last two years. It's now worth $260,000. We can get an interest-only first and second mortgage for almost all of that.

Nicole: You know how much we love Hawaii. We've got our eye on a property there. We'd like to use it for two weeks a year and have the management company rent it out the rest of the time. Do you think we can manage that?

Aaron: Absolutely! But you won't need to use much, if any, of the equity from your refinance to purchase your Hawaii property. You'll want to keep that equity separated to maintain liquidity, safety, and earn a rate of return. I'll show you how you can have a place in Hawaii with little to no monthly outlay on your part if you're going to rent it fifty weeks of the year. Let me run the numbers for you . . .

Isn't it worth a few extra hours of *your* time each month to progress toward financial freedom?

REMEMBER THIS

- You can obtain a second home or multiple real estate properties with little or no cash outlay and come out further ahead over time than if you allocated the same resources to an IRA or 401(k).
- Home equity, locked in the house, does not contain the three elements of a prudent investment: liquidity, safety, and rate of return.
- The rate of return on home equity is always zero.
- Refinance your mortgage as often as is feasible to separate and manage your equity to better increase liquidity, safety, and rate of return.
- Make money through the magic of positive leverage by exploiting the small differences between the tax-deductible mortgage interest rate you pay and the rate of return your separated equity can earn in liquid, safe investments.
- Don't wait; buy your second home and start acquiring multiple properties using the same strategies you used to buy your first home.
- Acquiring multiple properties and managing your real estate equity successfully is the key to accumulating a net worth in excess of $1 million by your thirties, which can then earn more than you do by working at a job.

LEARNING LINKS

Visit www.MissedFortune.com/Millionaire-By-Thirty and click on the learning portal for chapter 7 to:

- Listen to an audio recording that summarizes what you will learn in my book *Missed Fortune 101*.
- View a video stream containing highlights of my public

seminar titled "Missed Fortune True Wealth Transformation" that teaches about equity management.

- View a video stream using the "working metaphor" of a pitcher and glass (bottle and cup) illustrating why equity has no rate of return.

- Listen to an audio recording about how to establish an "Individual Retirement Abode (IRA)–401 Cabin or Condo" by investing in your second home and retirement savings at the same time.

- Download a special study issued by the Federal Reserve Bank of Chicago titled "The Tradeoff Between Mortgage Prepayments and Tax-Deferred Savings" that supports the strategies taught in this chapter.

- Use Emron and Aaron's Wealth Scenario Generator. By inserting some basic data in it, you will be guided on what price house you can afford with different types of mortgages and how you might separate equity from the house and invest it in a side fund.

- See how you take equity out of a house using a mortgage and invest it to generate wealth by borrowing at one rate and investing at the same or different rate.

- Review how to use the magic of compound interest, tax-free accumulation, and safe, positive leverage with various mortgages to generate as much as $1 million or more in assets, starting with your first home.

- Help determine how you can use a deferred-interest loan properly or what type of mortgage can provide you the greatest liquidity, safety, and rate of return to accelerate your wealth.

- Study examples of how you might manage your equity in multiple properties, including rental real estate.

CHAPTER 8

Think Smart Now, Retire Smart Later

Choose the Best Retirement Planning Investment Vehicles

NOT LONG AGO, A *NEW YORK TIMES* article issued this stark warning: "Even though most young workers realize that they're on their own when it comes to saving for retirement, many of those investing in 401(k)s haven't a clue how to allocate their funds."*

Perhaps you have a tough time envisioning yourself playing golf every day or reclining in a beach chair. On the other hand you have many years ahead of you. Imagine now that you've accumulated serious cash through managing the equity in your real estate properties. By refinancing as often as you can, you have used the magic of *thrust*—tax-free accumulation—to accumulate a million-dollar net worth by your thirties. A substantial portion of that is liquid and safely tucked in side funds. What do you do with it?

The quick answer is: you *optimize* it to produce wealth *that can last into perpetuity*.

---

* Paul J. Lim, "Youth Is Wasted on the Generation Y Investor," *New York Times*, March 19, 2006.

This gives you wonderful options for how to spend your older adult years. You can switch careers, travel, volunteer full-time for a charity or cause that you care about, or choose another exciting way for you and your loved ones to spend your time. You may not want to retire in the conventional sense, but you won't be dependent on the money you collect as salary. Your money is working for you.

You are in command, regardless of what life throws at you. If you are laid off or derailed by a family emergency, you are not lost. Occasionally even the best quarterbacks get sacked. But if you're Peyton Manning, you can throw a great pass to drive your team toward the end zone despite the temporary setback.

Here's the key. Your options include:

- You can figuratively *crawl* toward your later-life goals using typical savings plans.
- You can *walk* using tax-deferred annuities, stocks, bonds, or mutual funds.
- You can *jog* using traditional retirement programs such as IRAs and 401(k)s approved by the federal government.
- You can *sprint* to those goals using a private, liquid retirement program, which allows you to use your money tax-free—without the age barriers that shackle government-qualified plans that charge penalties for early withdrawal.

Sometimes it seems as though the race to financial freedom is awfully confusing. We would like to clear it up for you.

Would You Rather Crawl, Walk, Jog, or Sprint?

Back in chapter 2 we talked about this: If you were a farmer, would you rather be taxed on the money you use for seed at the start of your life, or on the profits of the harvest later in life?

This is the dilemma at the heart of most "qualified" (federal

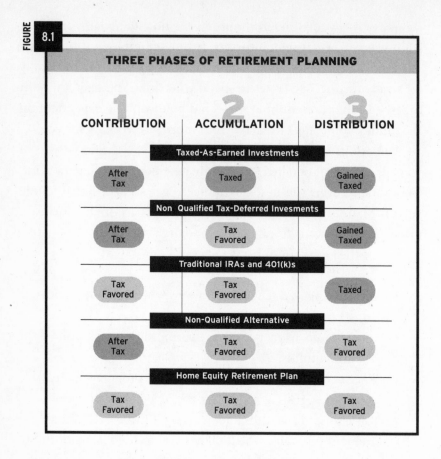

FIGURE 8.1

government–approved) retirement savings plans. In terms of a race to reach a million dollars, there are three stages—*contribution, accumulation*, and *distribution*. And there are different ways of reaching the finish line.

Those who save the old-fashioned way—putting their hard-earned saved dollars in passbook savings or interest-bearing checking accounts, money market accounts, or certificates of deposit—must *crawl*.

What about people who invest their after-tax dollars in stocks, mutual funds, bonds, or other investments? It may look like you are making a lot of money when the stock market is bullish, but *you've got to pay either capital gains taxes or income tax on your gains*. In other words, you are taxed as you earn the profits. Your returns will be diminished by the tax liability. What looks like a great leap forward in a bull market is really a *walk*.

Some of you may also be putting your extra dollars in deferred annuities. It sounds like a good idea, but that's really also a *walk*, as we will demonstrate later in this chapter.

Many of you may be contributing to an IRA or a 401(k) plan at work. If so, your contributions and accumulations are *tax-deferred*. You will eventually pay when you start collecting that money (the distribution phase). That's a *jog*.

What if you have been listening to exciting talk generated by the so-called Roth 401(k) or Roth IRA? We'll talk more about these in a moment. But the fact is, you pay up front on your money, even though the money you access later in life is tax-free. That's a *jog*, too, although with the wind at your back at the end of the race.

So how about winning the race, in the best of all possible worlds? How about a plan where you contribute money in a tax-favored environment, you accumulate the money the same way, and access it tax-free as well? That's a *sprint*.

Please look at the illustration below. Which lane on the track to retirement savings would you like to be in?

Ryan: Well, Aaron, as you know, Sarah and I finally bought a house and financed it with a mortgage. And you'll be pleased to hear that I started a retirement plan at work. My employer has a 401(k) plan and he matches 50 percent of what I contribute. Sarah, as a self-employed fashion designer, has started an IRA for us, too.

Aaron: That's a good start, Ryan. What does your dad think?

Ryan: My dad gets a pension from his company. He just hit sixty-two and decided to start collecting Social Security early. But he knows that these days, many companies have eliminated

FIGURE 8.2

pension plans. So he thinks an IRA or 401(k) is the next best thing.

Aaron: I gather you and Sarah want to start a family soon. What happens when the cash that is now discretionary for you—the cash that you sock away—is needed for baby expenses? You know, the bassinette, the clothes, stroller, car seat, the babysitter, the doctor . . .

Ryan: No problem. We'll just borrow from the retirement plans and pay them back later. That's allowed, according to my company benefits manager. After all, we won't need that money until years from now.

Aaron: Are you aware that when you withdraw or borrow money from an IRA or 401(k), there could be penalties? The most common is the IRS penalty of 10 percent when you withdraw money before you are fifty-nine and a half or borrow it without repaying it.

Ryan: Really? I didn't know about that part. Maybe we won't withdraw from our 401(k) or IRAs until we hit the so-called retirement age. I'm told at fifty-nine and a half we can start taking some money out of it.

Aaron: Did you know that when you do hit retirement age, if you do withdraw some of that money, you pay income tax on it?

Ryan: I think I heard something about that. And I know that Uncle Sam bites you even when you retire—that happened on my dad's pension and now even his Social Security. But you know what? That's more than thirty years down the road. I'll cross that bridge when I come to it.

Perhaps you remember Ryan, the finance major, from chapter 1. In just a moment, we'll help Ryan see how he and Sarah can sprint, rather than jog. We'll incorporate Emron and Harmony in the examples, and we'll introduce Jennifer, who is single and has been offered a chance to jog with the wind at her back at the end of the race. But before we get to that, let's understand a little more about IRAs, 401(k)s, and Roths.

Should You Participate in Matching 401(k) Programs?

When older people talk about a pension, they might very well be talking about the defined-benefit retirement plan that used to be much more common among salaried workers than it is now. Unfortunately, defined-benefit pensions are fairly uncommon in the twenty-first century. They have gone the way of the typewriter and the adding machine.

Looking at 401(k)s

Today, if your company or institution offers you any pension, it is most likely a 401(k) program, named for the section of the federal tax code that gave these programs tax-advantaged status.

A 401(k) allows you to contribute a portion of your salary before it is taxed to a fund where your money (plus any gains it accrues) grows without being taxed. In some instances, but not all, employers match your contributions either partially or 100 percent. Often you are not immediately eligible to participate in such plans. The idea is to help you save for retirement—but also to lock you in "golden handcuffs" designed to keep you at the same company.

Matching benefits may be useful, but you need to analyze them carefully, since they have some restrictions and there is no single formula. In some cases, employees contribute the maximum amount allowed under law, while the employer kicks in less than 100 cents on the dollar. True matching occurs when an employer agrees to match dollar for dollar on a percentage of an employee's income. To get the most out of matching, it is typically in your best interest to contribute at least the amount or percentage required to qualify for full matching benefit. After all, the matching dollars are "free."

However, note that the money is tax-*deferred*. That's not the same as *tax-free*. If you draw on your 401(k) before you reach age fifty-nine and a half, you must pay the taxes, plus a 10 percent IRS penalty! After age fifty-nine and a half, you can pull money out without penalty—but you still pay taxes on any withdrawals. That can add up to a lot of cash!

If you already have an IRA or 401(k), you may be permitted to withdraw money from it without penalty to assist you in getting into your first house.* This may help you when you need cash for a down payment. But the maximum you can withdraw is $10,000, and you must use the money within 120 days.† This can be a resource for a first-time homebuyer, but you cannot do it for any subsequent house you buy. It is best to check with your financial advisor and/or your accountant before taking this step.

Today's 401(k)s have safeguards that your parents' old-fashioned pensions did not. The assets in these programs are held in trust for

---

* http://www.irs.gov/retirement/article/0,,id=162415,00.html.
† http://moneycentral.msn.com/content/Taxes/P82396.asp.

you, in a separate account, so in case your employer goes bankrupt or gets entangled in corporate swindles, the company cannot touch your 401(k) holdings. Also, you can take the assets with you when you leave that particular job. But there are also drawbacks. A portion of the company contributions may be in the form of company stock. How awful can that sometimes be? Ask the former employees of Enron!

The best deal is at least a 50 percent matching benefit. But we still urge you to pay close attention before you channel pretax earnings into a 401(k). Be aware that your distributions will be taxed on the back end—your harvest years. All qualified plans have strings attached, and that is just one of them. For an in-depth analysis, see chapters 4 and 5 in *Missed Fortune 101* or chapter 9 in *The Last Chance Millionaire.*

Looking at IRAs and Roths

Every qualified plan—whether a 401(k), IRA, or the Roth version of either—is simply a tax-deferred retirement plan that is granted that status by the Internal Revenue Service. All come with strings attached. You are allowed to deposit only up to a certain limit each year, based on your age and income. You are subject to a 10 percent penalty if you withdraw money before you reach age fifty-nine and a half. If you borrow from it, you must repay it. As Aaron told Ryan, you are then replacing before-tax dollars with after-tax dollars, so you are somewhat penalized for that, too.

Let's emphasize the key point again: *Tax-deferred does not mean tax-free.* As is the case with a 401(k), when you have a traditional IRA, you pay tax once you start withdrawing money, during the distribution phase. What's more, you must start withdrawing money from an IRA and 401(k) at age seventy and a half. If you don't, Uncle Sam slaps you with a whopping 50 percent penalty on top of the tax.

As shown in figure 8.1, when you sock away money in quali-

One-size-fits-all advice?

fied accounts like IRAs or 401(k)s, your tax-deductible plan has a permanent tax lien attached that also grows. In other words, deferred taxes equal increased taxes. You may not think government is terribly efficient, but when it comes to getting its tax revenue, it becomes remarkably resourceful!

Jennifer: Say, Emron, my company has just started a Roth 401(k) plan. The benefits manager says this is way superior to the old 401(k). He's really pushing me to sign up for it. What do you think?

Emron: A Roth 401(k), like a Roth IRA, is somewhat better than a regular 401(k), but it still isn't the best choice. It will allow you to jog toward the finish line of retirement, but I can show you a plan that is genuinely "way superior"—a plan that's a *sprint*.

With Roth IRAs and Roth 401(k)s (named for the late Senator William V. Roth Jr.) the strings are loosened a bit. The income ceilings are a little higher in terms of how much you can contribute, and you do not have to withdraw a minimum amount at the age of seventy and a half. You contribute after-tax dollars to a Roth, meaning you pay taxes on the seed, so the distribution phase—the harvest—is tax-free. We think it is better to pay on the seed, but you are still not utilizing 100–cent dollars on both the front end and the back end of your retirement plan.

Wouldn't you prefer to have investment growth with *no tax at all*—using 100–cent dollars on the front end and enjoying 100–cent dollars on the back end?

That is what our private home equity retirement plan offers. Home equity retirement planning allows you to have three tax-advantaged circles—tax-favored treatment during the contribution phase, the accumulation phase, and the distribution phase. (As we've mentioned, there is a final phase, the transfer phase, which is when any money remaining is passed to your heirs.)

What's the catch? There is none. We simply utilize a *nonqualified* plan in which there are no limits, no required deposits, no age at which you must start withdrawals, and no IRS penalties for withdrawing at any age. When you have a terrific year you can contribute as much as you like. If you have an off-year financially, you do not have to contribute anything.

Our private plan allows you to have 50 percent *more* in net spendable retirement income or allows your income to last into perpetuity. Let's illustrate. Say that you have $1 million accumulated in a retirement nest egg by the time you are thirty-two, and it's earning 10 percent (to keep the math simple). How much could you withdraw every year and never deplete your $1 million nest egg? $100,000, right? Well, let's say that through time, due to inflation—the cost of living increasing—you need $100,000 *net* to spend a year, whether it is to go on frequent vacations, buy a new car, send your kids to superior private schools, or support your aging parents.

With a $100,000 income, you would likely be in a 30–35 percent marginal tax bracket. To keep the math simple, say you paid one-third of that income in tax. How much more would you have to withdraw so that after paying tax, you could net $100,000 to spend? That's right, 50 percent more. At that rate, how long will your million-dollar nest egg last? Only eleven years. So if you start to pull out $150,000 at thirty-two, your nest egg would be totally drained by age forty-three.

People who pay tax during the harvest years often face the danger of outliving their money—and that's not a happy future to imagine.

We don't want you to paint yourself into a corner with IRS-formatted retirement plans. We want you to get off on the right foot and then sprint to a stress-free financial future. We want your money to last into perpetuity.

Let's look at how a crawl, walk, jog, and sprint make Emron and Harmony's future look, and contrast that with how Ryan and Sarah's, and then Jennifer's, futures might turn out. (Not coincidentally, Ryan and Sarah's scenario may be the kind of stressful future your parents are facing.)

Ryan and Sarah both work and have a combined income that puts them in a 25 percent tax bracket. They decide up front to sock away at least 10 percent of their income. Because they don't know where else to save it, they put $7,000 a year into their IRA/401(k) plans. By earning 8 percent interest, Ryan and Sarah will end up with $856,421 in thirty years for retirement. At the same 8 percent interest, they can access $68,513 a year without depleting their account. Since they used an IRA/401(k), their entire withdrawal of $68,513 is subject to tax. Assuming they are already in a 25 percent tax bracket, they will have a net after-tax withdrawal of $51,385.

Jennifer is single and teaches third grade at a private school. She also falls in the 25 percent tax bracket. With her living expenses currently low, Jennifer is putting away $5,250 into her Roth 401(k)/Roth IRA earning 8 percent. This is the equivalent of Ryan and Sarah's $7,000 pretax contributions. After the same thirty years Jennifer will have $641,315 in her retirement account. *But her money will be tax-free.* Assuming she also continues to earn 8 percent, Sarah will also experience a net income of $51,385 without depleting her account.

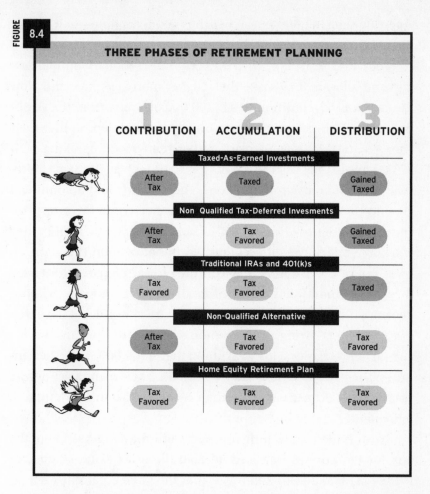

FIGURE 8.4

THREE PHASES OF RETIREMENT PLANNING

	1 CONTRIBUTION	2 ACCUMULATION	3 DISTRIBUTION
Taxed-As-Earned Investments	After Tax	Taxed	Gained Taxed
Non Qualified Tax-Deferred Invesments	After Tax	Tax Favored	Gained Taxed
Traditional IRAs and 401(k)s	Tax Favored	Tax Favored	Taxed
Non-Qualified Alternative	After Tax	Tax Favored	Tax Favored
Home Equity Retirement Plan	Tax Favored	Tax Favored	Tax Favored

In contrast, if Emron and Harmony (also in a 25 percent tax bracket) have the same $7,000 per year before tax ($5,250 after tax) to allocate toward retirement savings, they look to see how they could best optimize that money.

They just sold their starter home and moved into a new home closer to work. They were able to get $100,000 above what they owed on their previous mortgage from the sale of their home. Instead of putting that money into their new home in the form of a larger down payment, they decided to take out a larger mortgage instead. By using a $100,000 higher mortgage for their new home at a 7 percent interest rate, the extra $100,000 of mortgage proceeds is costing them $7,000 a year, which is tax-deductible—so it is only costing them a net of $5,250 after tax.

They choose to take their $7,000 of discretionary annual savings and allocate it to make their higher mortgage payment. Now they are able to reposition their $100,000 of equity from the sale of their former home and do a one-time lump-sum deposit into their "home equity retirement plan" rather than plodding along with $7,000 annual deposits to an IRA or 401(k). Over the same thirty years, Emron and Harmony's home equity retirement account will grow to the sum of $1,006,265. Because they chose the proper investment account (which we will explain in chapter 9), their money is tax-free not only as it accumulates, but also when they take income out of it. Assuming they continue to earn 8 percent interest, they can withdraw tax-free income of $80,501 annually without depleting their account. In this example, they would still have that extra $100,000 owing on their mortgage. So after paying the net annual mortgage cost of $5,250 on that $100,000, their net annual retirement income would be $75,251. Their spendable income is essentially 50 percent more than Ryan and Sarah's or Jennifer's retirement!

So all it took was a little ingenuity and thinking outside of the box for Emron and Harmony to take the exact same amount of money ($7,000 a year) and invest it at the same 8 percent interest, but end up with 50 percent more net spendable income. You can do this too.

Which Investments Meet the "LASER" Test for Your Retirement Plan?

Money that is earmarked for your future or your retirement is what we call "serious cash." We don't want to jeopardize it. So whenever we reposition serious cash, we want to make sure the investment vehicle passes the tests that home equity fails—the "LASER" test of liquidity, safety, and rate of return.

That's the first test. Any tax-favored benefits become icing on

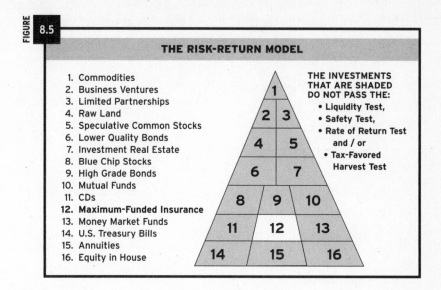

FIGURE 8.5

THE RISK-RETURN MODEL

1. Commodities
2. Business Ventures
3. Limited Partnerships
4. Raw Land
5. Speculative Common Stocks
6. Lower Quality Bonds
7. Investment Real Estate
8. Blue Chip Stocks
9. High Grade Bonds
10. Mutual Funds
11. CDs
12. **Maximum-Funded Insurance**
13. Money Market Funds
14. U.S. Treasury Bills
15. Annuities
16. Equity in House

THE INVESTMENTS THAT ARE SHADED DO NOT PASS THE:
• Liquidity Test,
• Safety Test,
• Rate of Return Test and / or
• Tax-Favored Harvest Test

the cake. And if we can have all of the above, we can have our cake and eat it too.

Numerous investments promise a high rate of return. Unfortunately, many also expose you to high risk. There are others that are safe, but they do not generate enough of a return to keep up with inflation over twenty or thirty years, so they would not be a great place for young adults to park their money.

You may have watched the popular reality TV show *Survivor* in which about twenty contestants vie for a million dollars. The contest eventually comes down to a "final three," and the one person who wins becomes the "sole survivor." The rest are castaways. In our financial practice, we identify sixteen general categories of investments ranked from highest risk to lowest risk, and most become castaways. Three do indeed make the final elimination round, yet only one qualifies on all counts to be our sole survivor.

In figure 8.5, you see our contestants. The ones at the top carry the highest risk, while the ones at the bottom carry the least risk. You probably have heard of several of them, while others may be new to you.

When we apply the *liquidity* test to our contestants, five fail:

- Business ventures
- Limited partnerships
- Raw land
- Investment real estate
- Equity trapped in your home

Why? You cannot get your money out of these quick enough in the event of an emergency.

Five more do not pass the safety test:

- Commodities
- Speculative common stocks
- Lower-quality bonds
- Blue-chip stocks
- Higher-grade bonds

Why? They are just too chancy.

Three more do not pass the *rate of return* test:

- Certificates of deposit
- Money market funds
- U.S. treasury bills

Why? They pay an interest rate so low that inflation often wipes out or exceeds any gains over a period of years.

As for what fails the *safety* test? Stocks. We know, finance professors, parents, and others may have touted stocks to you. But if you look at the performance of stocks over the past twenty-five years, you discover that investors scorned them in the 1980s, seized upon them in the 1990s, and were burned by them around the millennium. They simply don't cut it.

Only three investments remain. These "final three" can pass the liquidity, safety, and rate of return tests:

- Some mutual funds
- Some annuities
- Maximum-funded, tax-advantaged insurance contracts

Mutual Funds: Going Up, Going Down

Given the marketing might of mutual fund industry giants, this kind of investment is likely to be familiar to you. A mutual fund is where money is pooled together with lots of investors. The money is professionally managed by diversifying and attempting to have a rate of return over the long run that would be greater—with less risk—than investing in any one single stock.

Most funds will usually invest a large amount in growth stocks. So the returns can be volatile. You can lose 30 percent during the bad years, but maybe you can gain 35 percent in the really good years. The average increase from 1980 until 2000 was about 500 percent, meaning if you invested $10,000 it would grow to $50,000. That sounds pretty impressive, but it's really only an 8.38 percent average annual return.

During the 1990s you could have chosen mutual funds by throwing a dart at a board made up of newspaper clippings of the thousands of mutual funds now available, and if you had bought and held diversified funds, you would have earned an average of 13.9 percent.* Sounds great, doesn't it?

Unfortunately most people buy and sell funds, trying to time the market. So the average stock fund investor return between 1984 and 2001 in America was only about 4 percent,† because people

---

* http://www.fool.com/mutualfunds/indexfunds/indexfunds01.htm.

† http://www.astraea.net/holonics/economist/fundmanagement/fundmgmtaverages.html.

typically are holding investments for less than three years[*]—buying at the wrong time and selling at the wrong time.

What's more, even when the market in general goes up over a long term, there will be many peaks and valleys in the short run. It's like a person with a yo-yo walking up a flight of stairs. That's not an image that suggests safety, is it?

Rather than put money directly in the market, with its gyrations, it would be far better to reposition serious cash in less volatile investments.

With thousands of U.S. and international mutual funds to choose from, some do meet all three tests of liquidity, safety, and rate of return. But for serious cash, you would want to get the highest return at the lowest risk. That means you need to know what your risk tolerance is.

If you don't mind a slightly elevated risk, you might be willing to invest in a mutual fund aiming for good performance in a growth environment, versus one aimed at performing well in an income environment. So-called "growth stock" mutual funds may fluctuate considerably within a given period of time, while climbing over the long term. So-called "income" funds would include bonds, money markets, and other financial instruments that primarily generate income or dividends for use in the immediate future.

"Index" funds are structured to match the return of a well-known market gauge, such as the S&P 500 Index (which includes five hundred stocks that represent 70 percent of all U.S. publicly traded companies)[†] or the broader Wilshire 5000 Index (which includes practically all of the publicly traded companies that have U.S. headquarters).[‡]

Yet even one of the biggest diversified mutual funds, the Vanguard Total Stock Market Index fund, whose goal is to track the performance of the Wilshire 5000 Index and thus take into account

[*] http://www.soho.org/Finance_Articles/chasing_performance.htm.
[†] http://www.fool.com/school/indices/sp500.htm.
[‡] http://www.fool.com/school/indices/wilshire5000.htm.

the return of the overall stock market, does not do as well as you might expect.

From 1996 through 2005, the fund had seven gain years and three loss years. During the loss years, the value of the portfolio declined substantially—over 10 percent in two cases and over 20 percent in one. The loss years at first seem to be more than offset by the gain years, and the fund recorded an average return of about 9 percent. *However, anytime you experience a 10 or 20 percent loss in a fund that has grown to a sizable amount, you actually lose a major amount of money*, because the fund's value grew tremendously in the years before the losses occurred.

One problem with having a qualified retirement plan invested in a fund like this is that you must pay taxes once you start withdrawing the money. That slices a big chunk out of any gains. Also, recovering from market downturns can take one, two, three years or longer.

Often, investors—and not just youthful ones—look at the returns of a fund like this and see only the year-by-year history. They think they are getting a much higher return than they actually are. During the down years, they agonize over their losses. If, on the other hand, you have your investment return linked to the market without actually being in the market, you can do a lot better. And if you choose the right investments (which we will introduce shortly), you could very possibly withdraw money when you need to, totally tax-free.

If you want to review a detailed investigation of an investment in a taxable total stock market fund compared to an investment in a tax-free environment linked to the total market, see chapter 11 in *The Last Chance Millionaire*, the subsection titled "The Ups and Downs of Mutual Funds."

Figure 8.6 illustrates three different series of investments. Series 1 represents a taxable total stock market fund with direct participation *in* the market. Both Series 2 and 3 represent indexed funds that have their returns linked *to* the market without the money actually being at risk in the market. The Series 2 investment credits whatever Series 1 does up to a cap of 15 percent, but as a trade-off, it credits a minimum of 1 percent when the Series 1 fund loses money. Likewise, the Series 3 investment credits up to a cap of 12 percent and credits a minimum of 2 percent. *Please study the average returns indicated at the bottom of the chart—especially the net after-tax return.*

The real questions are, what would give you peace of mind when you are older—a more constant, stable return averaging 7, 8, or 9 percent compounded annually that is tax-favored during the harvest? Or a range of returns that might include some scary loss years? In other words, is the risk in mutual funds worth the reward? And how much of a meltdown will your gain suffer once you have to pay tax on it?

With mutual funds, whether you hold them in qualified tax-favored retirement plans or not, taxes must be paid—either on the front end or on the back end. With a fund in a traditional IRA or 401(k) account, the taxes are deferred in the contribution and ac-

FIGURE 8.6

STARTING WITH $100,000
If You Were Investing Serious Cash, Which Series Would You Prefer?

Year	SERIES 1 - TAXABLE TOTAL STOCK MARKET Indexed Value*		SERIES 2 - TAX FREE INDEXED VALUE* 15% cap 1% guarantee		SERIES 3 - TAX FREE INDEXED VALUE 12% cap 2% guarantee	
1	$120,960	20.96%	$115,000.00	15.00%	$112,000	12.00%
2	$158,446	30.99%	$132,250.00	15.00%	$125,440	12.00%
3	$195,300	23.26%	$152,087.50	15.00%	$140,493	12.00%
4	$241,801	23.81%	$174,900.63	15.00%	$157,352	12.00%
5	$216,242	-10.57%	$176,649.63	1.00%	$160,499	2.00%
6	$192,521	-10.97%	$178,416.13	1.00%	$163,709	2.00%
7	$152,168	-20.96%	$180,200.29	1.00%	$166,983	2.00%
8	$199,873	31.35%	$207,230.33	15.00%	$187,021	12.00%
9	$224,897	12.52%	$233,175.57	12.52%	$209,464	12.00%
10	$238,346	5.98%	$247,119.47	5.98%	$221,990	5.98%
Average Return		9.07%	Average Return	9.47%	Average Return	8.30%
Net After Tax Return		7.26%	Net After Tax Return	9.47%	Net After Tax Return	8.30%

*Fund Performance from 1996 through 2005

cumulation phases. But your money is taxed when you finally take out any of it. In a qualified Roth IRA or 401(k), as well as certain tax-free or tax-exempt bond mutual funds, you don't pay taxes when you access your money in your older years, but you are contributing taxed dollars on the front end.

What About Annuities?

We know that many young adults in certain professions such as teaching are often pitched annuities as a safe investment for retirement money.

Annuities are simply savings accounts with insurance companies. Because insurance companies have high legal reserve requirements, they are even less prone to failure than banks.

When you buy a traditional annuity, the insurer promises to pay you a specific amount of money over a period of time when it is annuitized. Many people sock away money into annuities with after-tax dollars, but annuities can be set up as a qualified plan with the choice of monthly income during retirement: over a set number of years or for the rest of their lives.

There are three basic types of annuities:

1) Fixed
2) Variable
3) Indexed

In each group there are two kinds of annuities: immediate and deferred. A retirement plan typically utilizes tax-deferred annuities.

Money deposited in a *deferred* annuity accumulates in a tax-favored environment. Even if it is not a qualified plan (i.e., IRS-approved), the money grows tax-deferred. A *fixed* annuity pays a rate of return based on the general account portfolio of the insurance company, although the return can fluctuate.

With a *variable* annuity, your return is based on the performance of the underlying stocks, bonds, or money market fund.

An *indexed* annuity's return is linked to one of the common market indices such as the S&P 500. With these indexed annuities, you do get a minimum guaranteed return even if the market goes down, and you benefit indirectly in any gains in the market, up to a ceiling or cap. The interest credited to you fluctuates according to the index to which it is linked.

Here again, the trouble is that with deferred annuities, as in a qualified retirement plan, if you want to withdraw the money before age fifty-nine and a half (for an emergency, layoff, job switch, vacation, etc.), you must pay a penalty and taxes. And after age fifty-nine and a half, money withdrawn still is taxable.

When you begin to withdraw money out of a *deferred* annuity, you have to pay tax on all of the interest first. This is called LIFO (last in, first out) tax treatment. In other words, the last money you are earning—your interest—is the first money you are taking out, as far as the IRS is concerned. And Uncle Sam collects taxes on it.

An immediate annuity begins paying you a certain amount right away, or within one year. You probably have noticed that in earlier chapters we talked about stashing money in a side fund. We often suggest that a good, safe side fund in which to park your money for a relatively short time can be a *single premium immediate annuity* (SPIA).

How does a SPIA work? You make one lump-sum deposit in such an annuity, and then collect immediate income distribution. The taxable portion of the annual distribution is averaged during the period the annuity is calculated to pay out.

During the past thirty years, fixed annuities have credited between 5 and 9 percent interest, for an average of about 7 percent. *That results in a net after-tax return of about 5 percent including administrative expenses.* This meets our test for a decent rate of return.

Some investors buy *variable* annuities whose goal is to get tax-deferred growth by using a variety of mutual funds. You can assign your variable annuity to the mutual fund management team of your choice. There may also be insurance within such an annuity. The price for this added protection is found in the annual expense charge, which could be approximately 2.25 percent of assets.

We think variable annuities are not necessarily the best choice for your home equity—there is just too much risk.

A Word About Indexed Annuities

If you are comfortable with some risk and you believe that the liquidity and rate of return on annuities meets your objectives, you can investigate *indexed annuities*. These allow you to participate *indirectly* when the market goes up, without the inherent risk incurred when money is actually *in* the market.

That's because indexed annuities contain a safety net, or guaranteed minimum interest rate. They will credit this rate regardless of what the market does, thus offering protection of principal. Your return is linked to an index such as the Dow Jones or Standard and Poor's.

In any event, there is an even better place than annuities for you to invest your serious cash when you want your money to be tax-free during every phase.

If you want to understand more about investment choices, please consult chapter 9 in *Missed Fortune 101* or chapter 17 in *Missed Fortune* for a more detailed explanation.

So Which Investment Is the Sole Survivor?

At this point, two of the "final three" investment categories we have discussed—some mutual funds and some annuities—lose out because their harvests are taxable. Why postpone taxes until later? How about just plain tax-free?

If we apply the "LASER" test and we aim for a tax-free harvest, there's only one sole survivor—one investment that you can use to contribute to, accumulate, and distribute money tax-free in your *sprint* toward the future: a *maximum-funded, tax-advantaged insurance contract.* The next chapter introduces this remarkably prudent, amazingly flexible investment.

REMEMBER THIS

- IRAs and 401(k)s may *not* be the best savings vehicles for retirement.
- In the "million-dollar dash" toward financial independence, rather than "crawl," "walk," or "jog" with the wind at your back at the beginning or end of the race, choose to "sprint" toward the finish line using a home equity retirement plan.
- You can experience 50 percent more in net spendable retirement income by using a home equity retirement planning strategy rather than putting money in traditional IRAs and 401(k)s or the Roth version of each.
- For serious cash, choose investments that pass the liquidity, safety, and rate of return "LASER" test.
- Among the investments that pass the "LASER" test, mutual funds can rack up great before-tax returns in some years, but can do poorly in other years, and they do not contain guarantees; fixed annuities contain some guarantees but are taxed when you access them; variable annuities are not stable enough.
- Only one investment passes the "LASER" test and allows you to enjoy tax-free harvests (tax-free retirement income): maximum-funded, tax-advantaged life insurance contracts—the sole survivor.

LEARNING LINKS

Visit www.MissedFortune.com/Millionaire-By-Thirty and click on the learning portal for chapter 8 to:
- Listen to an audio recording explaining how to solve the IRA/401(k) dilemma and understand why qualified retirement plans do not provide the most attractive retirement benefits.

- Listen to an audio recording explaining the success formula for choosing the right investments, structuring your life insurance to perform as a superior investment, and accessing your money tax-free at retirement.
- Register for one of many live webinars taught and broadcast via the Internet that teach asset optimization, equity management, and wealth empowerment.
- View a video stream explaining the difference between the "crawl," "walk," "jog," and "sprint" methods of accumulating money for retirement during the contribution, accumulation, and distribution phases of retirement planning.
- View a video stream explaining the "LASER" test as it is applied to various investments that eventually narrows those that pass all three tests to three finalists—only one of which allows you to enjoy tax-free harvests.

CHAPTER 9

Insure Your Future Financial Well-Being

Choose the Right Insurance

BY NOW YOU'RE HOPEFULLY ON BOARD with the power of buying a home and leveraging the equity to accelerate your financial momentum, but you may still be wondering about this life insurance thing. You're probably not alone.

Adam: Hey guys, I'm now seeing the value of a nonqualified retirement plan, and I have finally bought a house. But I just don't understand why you want me to buy insurance. When Heather and I get married next year, maybe I'll start saving money to buy some, but honestly, I don't expect to have a heart attack and die anytime soon.

Aaron: What if I showed you how to get Uncle Sam to pay indirectly for your life insurance with otherwise payable income tax?

Adam: Get out! The government doesn't do that.

Emron: I have over a million dollars of life insurance, and Uncle Sam is paying for it, indirectly. Along with the insurance itself, I've got a tax-favored retirement savings plan.

Aaron: The deal is that when you're young like us, insurance can be a two-for-one bonus. You get life insurance at an age where you might need it the most, and Uncle Sam actually rewards you for taking care of your family by *not* taking a tax bite.

Adam: Keep talking. I'm getting interested.

Like Emron's buddy Adam, you may think that life insurance is a luxury. Many young adults buy life insurance because their parents tell them they should have it for protection. But as soon as they have difficulty putting enough money in each budget envelope (category) every month, life insurance seems to be the most likely cost they can cut out. They view it as a negative.

So how come Emron and Aaron both have more than a million dollars of life insurance protection? First of all, they understand that they really need it at this point in their lives. And second, they understand how it can be the core of a great retirement savings plan in which actual insurance benefits come along for the ride. When structured correctly, they don't have to pay for it. Uncle Sam pays for it indirectly by granting tax-favored treatment to those who accept responsibility to protect and provide for their family, rather than relying on the government.

Before you started this book, you might have also perceived mortgage interest as a negative in your monthly budget. *But as we are about to demonstrate, these two supposed negatives—mortgage interest and insurance—can add up to a positive.*

Connect the Dots

As a kid, did you ever have an astronomy chart that taught you how to identify the constellations in the sky by connecting the dots? What we're about to do is connect the dots for you on this stellar financial strategy, to make you a millionaire by the time you are in your thirties.

First, we showed you how to buy your first home, then a second, and then multiple properties. We showed you how to turn the lazy, idle dollars trapped in your property into cash by using mortgages in order to separate equity from your house. Next, using Uncle Sam as your partner, we showed you how to generate savings on your taxes with deductible mortgage interest.

We suggested that you refinance a property as often as is feasible, and put the extra cash that results from refinancing into your private retirement savings plan. Each time you refinance, you save money in otherwise payable tax. You sock away that money in a prudent investment at a rate of return that might be the same as the rate on your mortgage or higher, and that also is tax-favored. This means you can use 100–cent dollars on the front end and enjoy 100–cent dollars on the back end.

Because you won't have to pay taxes when you accumulate or start withdrawing money from this nonqualified retirement plan, you achieve *arbitrage*—you make money on the small difference between the net mortgage interest rate and the net internal investment return rate.

Here's where we begin to connect the dots. Remember, the sole survivor in our contest (the one comparing different investments for serious cash) is *maximum-funded, tax-advantaged insurance contracts*. We'll refer to it as MFTA insurance for short, which could also mean "Missed Fortune Tax-Advantaged" insurance. Most people don't know you can use insurance as a cash accumulator. We're here to tell you it's a great Cash Accumulation Tool (CAT).

We will show you how to structure and fund certain MFTA insurance contracts that can credit 7, 8, or 9 percent a year and maybe even more.

Then we will show you how to access the money income-tax free in these insurance contracts a few years down the road.

This way, you can harvest more and more dollars from the small spread between the 6, 7, or 8 percent mortgage interest that is tax-deductible—thus having a net, after-tax cost of perhaps 4.5, 5.25, or 6 percent (in a 25 percent tax bracket)—and the interest you earn on the tax-favored insurance (perhaps 7, 8, or 9 percent). That creates a spread of between 2.5 to 3.0 percent between the interest rate you are earning on the tax-favored investment versus the rate of after-tax interest that you are paying. *The interest you are paying on the mortgage is simple interest, while the interest you earn on the insurance is compound interest, tax-free.* You will be able to generate 50 percent more income this way—an income that can last as long as you do.

What's more, you get life insurance protection for your loved ones. We will show you how to use otherwise payable income tax to cover the cost of your insurance benefits. Thus, with our strategy, Uncle Sam really pays for that coverage, indirectly.

We want to repeat this important point: *MFTA life insurance* is the *sole survivor* among the "final three" prudent investment categories. Unlike mutual funds or annuities, it allows you to have a tax-favored harvest. In other words, *it permits you to take your money tax-free on the back end, including all of your gains.*

Life insurance is the only choice that accumulates money tax-free, allows you to access your money tax-free, and when you die it doesn't just transfer tax-free, but it blossoms in value—meaning it possibly doubles, triples, quadruples, or more, and then transfers income-tax-free upon death to your heirs.

LINK TIP: For a set of sample plans and comparisons that show you how much better off you will be using MFTA life insurance as the core of your financial future savings plan, see our learning portal at www.MissedFortune.com/Millionaire-By-Thirty.

Most Americans, and even most financial consultants, do not realize they can get tax-advantaged life insurance contracts from the same top-rated life insurance companies that issue annuities.

They don't generally grasp the idea that these companies are not too different from a conservative mutual fund management company or banking institution.

This is part of our *systematic roadmap* toward financial independence in your thirties that we mentioned as an important keyword back in chapter 2. Make no mistake—*it runs contrary to the beliefs of conventional financial advisors.* However, we like to remind people that all the dogs barking up the same tree doesn't make it the right tree. Our approach can be considered the *opposite* of how many financial advisors and finance professors traditionally view life insurance, because instead of using it only for a death benefit, we use it for *maximum living benefits.*

A Quick Intro to Life Insurance

Most of our clients don't come to us necessarily wanting "insurance." They simply want a safe, liquid investment with a good rate of return, as well as tax-favored treatment of the distributions.

That's what MFTA insurance provides. Before explaining how it works, let's go through a fast but useful guide to life insurance.

Insurance is a trillion-dollar industry in the United States and probably one of the most stable sectors of the American economy. As experts in managing risk, insurance companies are responsible by law for investing money wisely to get a safe rate of return. So many life insurance companies invest their capital in a conservative portfolio primarily consisting of high-grade bonds. They tend to be less volatile than most mutual funds.

Until the 1980s, life insurance polices were not attractive as retirement planning vehicles because a typical whole life insurance policy may have credited only about 2.5 to 3.5 percent on the cash values that accumulated in them. But then innovative firms found a way to structure policies to produce a much *greater* rate of return—*averaging 6, 7, 8, or 9 percent.*

Please understand: We are *not* suggesting that you buy *stock* in insurance companies. If we urged you to put money in Wells Fargo Bank, we would be telling you to deposit your money there, not necessarily to buy stock in Wells Fargo. It's the same here: You are depositing money with insurance companies, which are conservative managers of money.

How much life insurance do you need? Risk managers recommend that young adults carry fifteen to twenty times their annual income in actual death benefit. Those of you who have one or two properties and dependents, such as a spouse and children (or those who will soon have a family), undoubtedly want to protect your assets and your loved ones in the unlikely event that you are not there to take care of them financially.

Right now, if you are making $50,000 a year, a $1 million death benefit is equal to twenty times your income. Once you reach your thirties and have accumulated a million-dollar net worth, that amount of money earning a conservative 7 percent rate of return could generate as much as $70,000 a year of income.

One of our clients not long ago succumbed to cancer. She was not yet forty years old, and she and her husband have several children. Young adults don't usually think much about accidents or illnesses that could cut them down in the prime of life, but they do happen.

The husband was the breadwinner, but he and his wife had bought life insurance to cover each of them individually. She had $400,000 worth of insurance. With that benefit, her grieving husband decided to stop working for a while and take care of his youngest child, who is only three, until he starts kindergarten. Imagine how different things would be if, after suffering such an incalculable personal loss, they did not have any cushion of money to fall back on.

Adam: So far you make sense. But look at my cousin David. He's free and single, and he has no plans to get married anytime soon. Why would he bother with life insurance?

Emron: MFTA insurance works as a tax-favored Cash Accumulation Tool—you could call it a phat *CAT* instead of a cash cow. We all could use that, at any stage of our lives. But what if David's employer came to him and said, "Hey, we have some additional benefits we're offering this year—free life insurance. How much would you like?" What would he reply?

Adam: I guess he'd say, "I'll take as much as I can get—if it doesn't cost anything!"

Aaron: That's what we're trying to show you—the cost of insurance can be covered by a small portion of the interest you earn that would otherwise be paid out in income tax if you were using other taxable investments. Hence, it's like Uncle Sam is indirectly letting you use otherwise payable income tax to offset the cost of the life insurance. Life insurance must be included, or the tax-free benefits would be forfeited. So, the insurance comes along for the ride when it is structured correctly—which means the least amount of life insurance required under IRS guidelines is taken out for the amount of money being invested. The rate of return is enhanced when the money is paid into the insurance contract within a five-year period and then allowed to grow tax-free until income is needed. At that point, the income can be taken through tax-advantaged methods.

When I was in my twenties and just getting started in financial planning, I had a client, a twenty-nine-year-old who lived in our neighborhood, whom we'll call Bob. I talked to Bob about a savings plan anchored by MFTA insurance. Bob resisted it.

"I'm insurance-poor," he said. "I don't need any more life insurance."

I managed to convince him that in his case, $250,000 worth of insurance came along with the financial plan I drew up. Bob took the required physical exam and was approved for the insurance. As he and I were filling out the forms, Bob coughed frequently and complained that he could not shake a cold.

The insurance was approved two days before Bob was diagnosed with Stage 4 Hodgkin's disease, a deadly cancer. His whole attitude changed. He then wanted to increase the insurance benefit, which was not possible, of course. Sadly, Bob lived just thirteen months longer.

The point is that no one really objects to insurance benefits. They just object to paying for it. If you take ownership in taking care of your dependents—if your survivors won't need to ask the federal government to bail them out—Uncle Sam gives you a break. That's just one of the reasons why insurance proceeds are tax-free.

LINK TIP: Go to www.MissedFortune.com/Millionaire-By-Thirty in the learning portal for background on insurance, plus explanations of sections 72e, 7702, and 101(a) of the Internal Revenue Code, as well as how changes since the 1980s make MFTA insurance a great cash accumulation vehicle. You can also read more about the tax code and the federal laws that govern their use in chapter 10 of *Missed Fortune 101*, chapter 17 of *Missed Fortune*, or Appendix A of *The Last Chance Millionaire*.

What Are the Different Kinds of Insurance?

There are two basic categories of life insurance: term insurance and cash-value or permanent insurance.

Term insurance refers to policies that provide only a death benefit. They are designed for people who want to pay the smallest premium possible, but they are not good cash accumulators for future financial freedom plans because they don't accumulate cash values and thus cannot produce living benefits.

Cash-value insurance provides a built-in savings component, as well as death benefits. These are the insurance contracts that can be structured to be the most prudent core vehicles in which to store cash for your retirement planning.

With a cash-value policy, the policyholder can pay an average premium over the term of the policy. The excess premium—what you pay over and above the costs of the death benefit or mortality charges and the sales and administration expenses—builds up cash value and *accumulates with interest*. This excess money then begins to accrue and you can then use it for living benefits.

As long as there is *some* life insurance attached to a policy, it qualifies as being *tax-favored* during the accumulation and distribution phases. These policies are also income-tax-free when passed along to heirs in the "transfer" phase. So, as long as it qualifies as a life insurance policy, a contract that is funded with a maximum amount of contributions can turn into a *phat CAT for retirement*. CAT is based on the ideas I outlined in my first book, *Missed Fortune*. Again, it is MFTA, or maximum-funded, tax-advantaged life insurance.

We call this the "back door approach," because instead of buying a certain amount of life insurance protection that will pay off if you die (where you want to pay the least amount of premium for that life insurance benefit), you're doing just the opposite.

With MFTA insurance, you get the *least amount of death benefit* that the tax code allows, which at younger ages is usually a considerable amount, while you *pay the most premium* that the IRS will allow, *so that your money will accumulate tax-free with the least amount of expenses*.

Kinds of Cash-Value Insurance Policies

It's easy to get confused about insurance policies because they come in what can be a bewildering variety of flavors. We're going to simplify this as much as possible. If you want a lengthier and more complete explanation including all of the math, you can refer to chapters 10 and 11 of *Missed Fortune 101*.

There are two kinds of cash-value policies:

- Whole life
- Universal life

We prefer what is typically called *universal* life, because it is the most flexible and generally performs better for retirement objectives.

Under the term "universal life" there are three versions:

1) Fixed
2) Indexed
3) Variable

The version of universal life that you choose for your future savings depends on how conservative you want your contract to be.

Remember back in chapter 3, we taught you that most people keep money that they set aside and accumulate for long-range goals in one of three lodging places:

- Low-risk, stable investments (houses of bricks)
- Moderate-risk investments (houses of sticks)
- Higher-risk investments (houses of straw)

In chapter 8, we identified MFTA insurance contracts as the most prudent investment—a house of bricks—in the entire risk versus reward pyramid because it passes the "LASER" test, offering liquidity, safety, and a good rate of return—while also offering you a tax-favored harvest. So all three of these universal life insurance choices can be prudent.

The most conservative choice here is the *fixed* universal life insurance contract. These generally have the lowest expense charges, too. "Fixed" means you get interest based on the insurance company's relatively fixed general account portfolio made up largely of high-grade bonds, with some money in mortgage-backed securities and a smaller amount in stocks, real estate, cash, and other short-term investments.

A fixed universal life policy typically has a guaranteed minimum interest rate, usually around 3 to 4 percent. We've observed that very few companies credit only the guaranteed rate. But you will know what the minimum is because the industry's rules mandate that you be shown—and sign off on—an illustration that projects both the current interest rate and the worst-case scenario on a policy's benefits.

The least conservative choice is the *variable* universal life contract. The difference between a variable universal life and a fixed contract is that all cash values except the amount needed to cover the cost of insurance and expense charges are invested—not in the insurance company's own portfolio, but in equities. There is no guaranteed minimum interest rate. If the investments suffer a loss and the portfolio does not contain sufficient cash, policy owners may have to make additional premium payments in order to make sure their cost of insurance and expense charges are covered.

In between fixed and variable is *indexed universal life*. This is the policy you might prefer if you want to be a little less conservative than fixed but earn a more stable return than variable. You keep your retirement savings in a house of bricks, and still participate *indirectly* in gains from a house of straw—the stock market—without your money actually lodged there.

With an indexed universal life insurance contract, your return is *linked* to an index like the S&P 500, Dow Jones, or Euro Stock Index. But you have not put your money at risk *in* the market. When the stock market goes down you don't lose, because indexed universal life contracts have a guaranteed floor of 1, 2, or 3 percent. When the market goes up, you benefit from its growth.

How to Build Your Future with MFTA Insurance

Let's look at another example of how this might work.

Jennifer: I'm a big fan of *Survivor*, guys. I'd like to hear more about how this insurance thing works. You're suggesting that your nonqualified plan is better than the 401(k) my company offers. How exactly do I get to my thirties and be the sole survivor with a million dollars?

Emron: We begin with the idea that an MFTA insurance contract is like a bucket, and we pour money into it.

Jennifer: Do I need a huge amount of money? I've only got $5,000 socked away right now in a certificate of deposit.

Aaron: What's great about being young is you have time to fill your bucket. When I took out my first contract, I was your age, and I decided on a bucket that would hold up to $85,000 over the next eleven years.

Jennifer: Wow, $85,000 over eleven years?

Emron: This is a long-term strategy, Jennifer, so you've got to be committed.

When we begin to save money in the house of bricks using MFTA insurance contracts, we still need to abide by certain IRS guidelines. We compare the process to filling up a bucket designed to accumulate cash. The money grows, thanks to the magic of compound interest. However, in order to comply with IRS guidelines and recent tax law, you need to fill up each bucket over a period of time with no more than a specified amount going into it each year, depending on the size of the bucket you establish.

Most people fill their buckets with cash during the first few years. The spigot on the bucket is the cost of the insurance. It is like drip irrigation—it waters a marvelous tree that ultimately will blos-

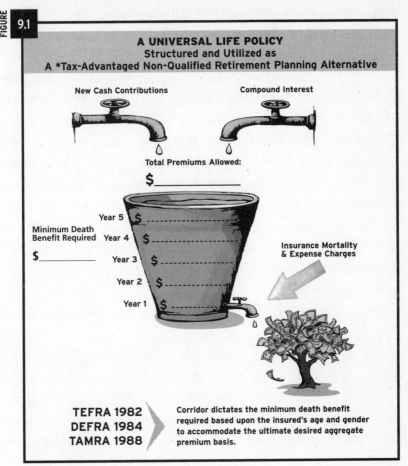

FIGURE 9.1

A UNIVERSAL LIFE POLICY
Structured and Utilized as
A *Tax-Advantaged Non-Qualified Retirement Planning Alternative

New Cash Contributions   Compound Interest

Total Premiums Allowed:

$_____

Year 5 $ _____

Minimum Death
Benefit Required   Year 4 $ _____

$_____   Year 3 $ _____

Year 2 $ _____

Year 1 $ _____

Insurance Mortality
& Expense Charges

TEFRA 1982
DEFRA 1984
TAMRA 1988

Corridor dictates the minimum death benefit
required based upon the insured's age and gender
to accommodate the ultimate desired aggregate
premium basis.

* *Tax Citations: IRC Section 101, IRC Section 72(e), Rev. Rul 66-322,*
1966-2 CB 123, Tefra Section 266, DEFRA Section 221

som and transfer your remaining balance income-tax-free to your heirs when you pass away.

By adhering to these federal laws, you can access your money income-tax-free after a few years, whether you want it as retirement income, or simply want enough money to pursue new pathways in your life when you are older. Various federal guidelines dictate the minimum death benefit based upon your age and gender. Because you are young, for every dollar you put in your first bucket, you will need to buy anywhere from $3 to $10 of life insurance. Remember, indirectly, Uncle Sam pays for it.

By following the guidelines, you can get by with the least amount of life insurance possible (which is still a lot for young people) so that the spigot on the bucket drains out the least amount of cost possible. (Incidentally, if you are not in good health or you are not insurable for one reason or another, you can use a surrogate life to insure, such as your spouse, children, or parents. It's the owner of the insurance contract who benefits from and is entitled to the tax-favored accumulation and tax-favored income.)

Once we find out if you are insurable and determine the amount of money you want to put in your bucket, we structure a plan that conforms to IRS rules. The guidelines allow you to achieve the same great rate of return, no matter what, by squeezing down the required death benefit to the minimum amount allowed based on your circumstances.

We recommend that you choose a fixed or indexed insurance contract based upon which ones will generate the most at the time in life you're likely going to need the money the most. Just as you should not park money in CDs and money markets for long-range goals like retirement, you don't use insurance contracts for short-term purposes.

For long-range goals, the best house of bricks is like a five-story building that you've constructed. Not until you fill up or rent out the first few floors do you earn more than the building is costing. When you fill up the second and third floors, you are able to offset most, if not all, of the costs associated with maintaining the building. When you have finally filled up the third floor (or it's 60 percent occupied), the rent income is usually covering your cost for the building. It is the same with a MFTA insurance contract. Once you have your bucket 60 percent filled, the earning on the cash value should be covering the insurance mortality and expense charges. The interest you are earning on the money deposited in the build-

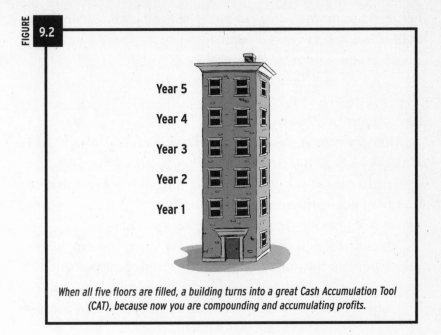

Year 5

Year 4

Year 3

Year 2

Year 1

When all five floors are filled, a building turns into a great Cash Accumulation Tool (CAT), because now you are compounding and accumulating profits.

ing is likely covering the cost of the insurance that has to be there, or it won't qualify as a tax-free cash accumulation vehicle.

When you have finally filled up the fourth and fifth floor, that's when a building turns into a phat CAT, because now you are compounding and accumulating profits. And if you let that positive cash flow compound and grow, it will experience an amazing rate of return, retroactive back to the first year—even though only one floor was occupied at that time.

Let's return to the bucket. When your bucket is only 20 percent full, the spigot on the bucket is going to drain out a bigger percentage than when it's 100 percent full. You must be patient as you fill up the bucket with your cash, so that the rate of return over the life of the policy, retroactive back to day one, comes within about 1 percent of the gross rate of return.

Imagine: You've taken lazy, idle dollars of equity and removed it from your properties. Now you've got $1 million in a MFTA insurance contract that's working for you and is earning a net internal rate of return of 6, 7, or 8 percent. Thus you have a savings plan from which you can peel off dollars to pay for your future, regardless of what you want to do next in life.

Next, Access Your Money Tax-Free

How can you access money out of an insurance contract? There are three ways: *the sad way, the smart way, and the dumb way.*

Briefly, the sad way is by dying. In the unlikely event that you pass away sooner than anticipated, the death benefit blossoms into a great deal of money to provide for your loved ones.

The smart way is this: For the first few years, you can pull out your basis (the total amount that you personally deposited). You are taking out what you put in, so under IRS guidelines, it's tax-free. How smart is that? It won't be deemed earned, passive, or portfolio income by the IRS, so it will be totally tax-free.

After a certain point, you would be withdrawing your interest, and in that case the IRS would tax the money. So after you have withdrawn your basis, the dumb way is to continue to withdraw the money, even though the IRS says it is within the law to *borrow* the money.

So after a certain number of years, you could borrow the same amount from the insurance company. When you do that, you are borrowing against the cash value in your contract. Since it is neither earned, passive, nor portfolio income, the money continues to be totally tax-free. The loan income can be structured to be taken with no net charge. This is called a zero wash or preferred loan. The loan is automatically paid off when a person ultimately passes away.

What's even more amazing is that given the money's tax-free status, this plan can last as long as you do—even if you live to age 150!

Remember Liz, the Super Thriver from chapter 7? Figure 9.3 illustrates her actual side fund—her insurance policy—that she used to generate her wealth. If you recall, Liz recently graduated from

FIGURE 9.3

TAX-FREE ACCESS VIA WITHDRAWALS AND LOANS

Age	Year	Premium Payment	Withdrawal or Loan Proceeds	Year End Accumulation Value	Year End Surrender Value	Death Benefit
23	1	$8,442	$0	$7,432	$6,754	$352,852
24	2	$8,442	$0	$15,594	$14,134	$361,014
25	3	$8,442	$0	$24,525	$22,197	$369,945
26	4	$75,263	$0	$93,022	$79,215	$4,053,482
27	5	$63,578	$0	$156,959	$130,983	$4,117,418
28	6	$8,442	$0	$173,964	$150,997	$4,134,423
29	7	$130,375	$0	$310,185	$274,330	$4,270,644
30	8	$75,985	$0	$406,614	$360,691	$4,367,073
31	9	$72,579	$0	$508,793	$462,870	$4,469,252
32	10	$298,186	$0	$838,433	$792,510	$4,798,892
33	11	$0	$55,000	$908,966	$744,800	$4,739,652
34	12	$0	$55,000	$984,232	$756,982	$4,675,842
35	13	$0	$55,000	$1,064,530	$769,272	$4,607,108
36	14	$0	$55,000	$1,150,177	$782,541	$4,534,005
37	15	$0	$55,000	$1,241,609	$805,404	$4,456,252
38	16	$0	$55,000	$1,339,115	$829,393	$4,376,999
39	17	$0	$55,000	$1,443,081	$853,847	$4,325,350
40	18	$0	$55,000	$1,553,938	$879,579	$4,270,346
41	19	$0	$55,000	$1,672,129	$906,672	$4,211,761
42	20	$0	$55,000	$1,798,219	$926,846	$4,131,983
43	21	$0	$55,000	$1,932,498	$948,435	$4,045,664
44	22	$0	$55,000	$2,075,538	$983,370	$3,952,322
45	23	$0	$55,000	$2,227,940	$1,019,988	$3,851,440
46	24	$0	$55,000	$2,390,201	$1,058,281	$3,830,615
47	25	$0	$55,000	$2,562,998	$1,098,394	$3,903,861
52	30	$0	$55,000	$3,607,162	$1,279,940	$4,093,526
57	35	$0	$55,000	$5,036,474	$1,513,546	$3,830,323
62	40	$0	$55,000	$7,007,570	$1,847,004	$3,809,123
67	45	$0	$55,000	$9,714,647	$2,307,430	$4,153,214
72	50	$0	$55,000	$13,426,345	$2,931,606	$4,677,031
77	55	$0	$55,000	$18,623,999	$3,878,453	$4,809,653
82	60	$0	$55,000	$25,821,189	$5,212,245	$6,503,302
87	65	$0	$55,000	$35,578,067	$6,865,649	$8,644,550
92	70	$0	$55,000	$48,630,264	$8,696,053	$10,641,264
97	75	$0	$55,000	$67,599,207	$12,093,029	$12,093,029
100	78	$0	$55,000	$82,816,275	$15,184,925	$15,184,930

TOTAL $749,734   **$3,740,000**

Assuming a 9.18 percent gross interest crediting rate.

college and had an income of $50,000. Originally all she could afford to set aside was 3 percent of her income ($103.87 after tax) to her bucket. But after freeing herself from throwing money away in rent and repositioning that monthly outlay to buying a home, she was able to find a way to save 17 percent of her income. She did this by taking out an interest-only mortgage rather than a thirty-year mortgage and saving the difference in payments. She also took her new tax savings from her mortgage and the extra money she was using to pay down her student loan and began paying herself first by putting that money into her bucket. This gave her a total of $703.52 per month for the next ten years to deposit into her bucket. So initially Liz opens up a bucket to hold a maximum premium of $8,442 per year as seen in year one of figure 9.3. This gives her an initial minimum death benefit of $352,852 under the IRS rules. Even though at first Liz thinks that she may not need that much life insurance, she understands that $352,852 (in this case) is the minimum death benefit if she wants to deposit as much as $702.52 a month into an MFTA insurance policy. The death benefit is, in essence, coming along for the ride.

Remember that Liz also learned how to repeat the process and bought four additional homes and rented them. She began refinancing and repositioning the equity from her real estate properties in the fourth year and continued to do so every two to four years thereafter. She deposited those mortgage refinance proceeds into a new bucket that she started in year four. So she set up a second bucket to accommodate a total of $580,405 in deposits over six years. This gave her a minimum death benefit of $3,673,753, which she split between herself and her husband. So beginning in year four, between the two buckets, Liz will ultimately deposit a total of $749,734, which will require a combined total death benefit of $4,053,482 between the two policies (see figure 9.3, year 4).

After Liz turns age thirty-two, just ten years after starting to optimize assets and successfully manage equity, she has $838,433 accumulated in her bucket. If she decided to, she could then begin taking a tax-free income of $55,000 a year forever and never deplete the money in her buckets based on an average gross crediting rate of 9.18 percent annually (which is what would have been achieved during the twenty-five-year period ending 2007 based on the actual performance of the S&P 500 Index using a model of a 1 percent floor and a 15 percent cap). That is more than the $50,000 of income she was earning by working in a job that she still has to pay taxes on. Because Liz takes her money out the smart way, via tax-free loans, her account continues to grow so that at age sixty-seven she has a net of $2,307,430. At age eighty-two she has $5,212,245. And at age 100 she has $15,184,925.

Please don't be intimidated by this example if the size of this first bucket is more than you have on hand right now. You could create a small bucket that would only accommodate a total of $5,000; or one big enough to hold $100,000; or you could design a bucket that will accommodate $5 million. It doesn't make any difference. You create a bucket that will accommodate the amount you think you're likely going to reposition or save within the next five to ten years, and then it makes sense for you to deposit that money as soon as possible in compliance with guidelines set by the government.

Here's the bottom line:

Liz is currently twenty-two years old. By structuring her buckets properly and adhering to IRS guidelines, by age thirty-two she can have a plan potentially earning a gross average return of about 9 percent. That means her and her husband have just shy of $1 million accumulated by the tenth year in a financial freedom plan that can generate more income than she does from working at her job. They can have over $4 million in death benefits coming along for the ride. The cost of the insurance itself after a certain period of time only consumes about 1 percent of the gross return. Therefore, if they were to average 9 percent in gross interest, they could have a net internal rate of return, cash-on-cash, of about 8 percent (net after the cost of the insurance). Likewise, if they were to average 8 percent in gross interest, they could have a net internal rate of return, cash-on-cash, of about 7 percent. The 1 percent difference is what pays for the amount of life insurance that the IRS guidelines dictate have to be included, or it would not qualify as a tax-advantaged life insurance contract.

Comparing This to Other Alternative Investments

Now let's take a quick look at what would have happened if Liz had chosen a certificate of deposit earning 5.5 percent interest, an annuity earning 8.5 percent, a mutual fund averaging 9.18 percent in annual growth, or an IRA/401(k) growing at 9.18 percent. As you can see in figure 9.4, we have listed these different investment alternatives, by hypothetically depositing the same amount of money into each over the same ten-year period—displaying the after-tax equivalent value for each option. Glancing at year ten, it may look like some of these alternative options are going to outperform the insurance policy. But a smart planner knows that you do not choose long-term retirement accounts based on which one is going to grow to the most money. You choose the investment that is going to *generate* the most. So as the insurance policy can generate $55,000 of tax-free income every year in this example, all of the other alternatives are going to have to generate more to net the same $55,000 after paying taxes during the distribution phase. So when the certificate of deposit is depleted to its last dollars at age fifty-seven, the insurance policy still has over $1.5 million in it. The mutual fund is the next best competitor, but it still runs out of steam at age eighty-two when the insurance policy still has a net value of $5,212,245. All of these alternatives run out of steam and would go into negative territory in order to generate the same amount of net income as the maximum-funded, tax-advantaged life insurance policy. In this example, an MFTA life insurance contract can generate nearly $1 million or more than all of the other accounts by age 100, and instead of being depleted, it still has a net value of $15,184,925 at that point in time! And this is assuming that you remained in a low 20 percent tax bracket the entire time. If you jumped up to any higher tax bracket the gap would be even greater! Oh yeah, did we forget to mention that during all of this time you have a death benefit coming along for the ride? Will any of these other accounts blossom into several times its value if something were to happen to you? Not a chance. Properly structured MFTA life insurance is

FIGURE
9.4

INDEXED UNIVERSAL LIFE COMPARED TO VARIOUS ALTERNATIVES

	TAX TYPE	INTEREST RATE	MANAGEMENT FEE	PREMATURE DIST. TAX	SALES CHARGE
Certificate of Deposit	Taxable	5.50%	0.00%	0.00%	0.00%
Annuity	Deferred	8.50%	1.00%	10.00%	3.00%
Mutual Fund	Taxable	9.18%	1.00%	0.00%	3.00%
IRA/401(k)	Qualified 2	9.18%	1.00%	10.00%	0.00%
Indexed Universal Life	Tax Favored	9.18%			

		AFTER TAX VALUES				INSURANCE VALUES		
Year (Age)	Net Withdrawals or Payment	Certificate of Deposit	An Annuity	Mutual Fund	IRAs & 401(k)s	Accumulation Value	Surrender Value	Death Benefit
1 (23)	$8,442	$8,813	$8,690	$8,701	$6,387	$7,432	$6,754	$352,852
2 (24)	$8,442	$18,015	$17,836	$17,945	$13,291	$15,594	$14,134	$361,014
3 (25)	$8,442	$27,621	$27,473	$27,768	$20,754	$24,525	$22,197	$369,945
4 (26)	$75,263	$107,411	$106,418	$107,074	$79,378	$93,022	$79,215	$4,053,482
5 (27)	$63,578	$178,512	$177,516	$179,295	$133,902	$156,959	$130,983	$4,117,418
6 (28)	$8,442	$195,180	$195,716	$199,205	$151,120	$173,964	$150,997	$4,134,423
7 (29)	$130,375	$339,880	$340,590	$346,030	$261,987	$310,185	$274,330	$4,270,644
8 (30)	$75,985	$434,163	$437,320	$445,979	$340,668	$406,614	$360,691	$4,367,073
9 (31)	$72,579	$529,038	$536,026	$548,665	$423,137	$508,793	$462,870	$4,469,252
10 (32)	$298,186	$863,622	$872,665	$890,293	$682,973	$838,433	$792,510	$4,798,892
11 (33)	$-55,000	$844,201	$861,617	$887,518	$678,765	$908,966	$744,800	$4,739,652
12 (34)	$-55,000	$823,926	$849,750	$884,568	$984,232	$674,217	$756,982	$4,675,842
13 (35)	$-55,000	$802,759	$837,002	$881,435	$669,300	$1,064,530	$769,272	$4,607,108
14 (36)	$-55,000	$780,661	$823,310	$878,105	$663,986	$1,150,177	$782,541	$4,534,005
15 (37)	$-55,000	$757,590	$808,602	$874,567	$658,242	$1,241,609	$805,404	$4,456,252
16 (38)	$-55,000	$733,504	$792,804	$870,808	$652,033	$1,339,115	$829,393	$4,376,999
17 (39)	$-55,000	$708,358	$782,572	$866,814	$645,323	$1,443,081	$853,847	$4,325,350
18 (40)	$-55,000	$682,105	$771,140	$862,570	$638,069	$1,553,938	$879,579	$4,270,346
19 (41)	$-55,000	$654,698	$759,029	$858,061	$630,229	$1,672,129	$906,672	$4,211,761
20 (42)	$-55,000	$626,085	$746,200	$853,270	$621,754	$1,798,219	$926,846	$4,131,983
25 (47)	$-55,000	$462,988	$669,694	$824,429	$567,923	$2,562,998	$1,098,394	$3,903,861
30 (52)	$-55,000	$260,711	$567,641	$785,372	$488,504	$3,607,162	$1,279,940	$4,093,526
35 (57)	$-55,000	$9,841	$431,508	$732,481	$371,334	$5,036,474	$1,513,546	$3,830,323
40 (62)	$-55,000	$-301,296	$251,677	$660,854	$244,492	$7,007,570	$1,847,004	$3,809,123
45 (67)	$-55,000	$-687,177	$7,735	$563,855	$11,334	$9,714,647	$2,307,430	$4,153,214
50 (72)	$-55,000	$-1,165,760	$-341,966	$432,497	$-428,854	$13,426,345	$2,931,606	$4,677,031
55 (77)	$-55,000	$-1,759,312	$-867,795	$254,610	$-1,116,145	$18,623,999	$3,878,453	$4,809,653
60 (82)	$-55,000	$-2,495,454	$-1,658,463	$13,711	$-2,182,388	$25,821,189	$5,212,245	$6,503,302
65 (87)	$-55,000	$-3,408,440	$-2,847,356	$-322,316	$-3,836,526	$35,578,067	$6,865,649	$8,644,550
70 (92)	$-55,000	$-4,540,753	$-4,635,042	$-801,235	$-6,402,705	$48,630,264	$8,696,053	$10,641,264
75 (97)	$-55,000	$-5,945,083	$-7,323,109	$-1,483,812	$-10,383,800	$67,599,207	$12,093,029	$12,093,029
78 (100)	$-55,000	$-6,944,820	$-9,548,400	$-2,025,765	$-13,760,540	$82,816,275	$15,184,925	$15,184,930

$-2,790,543

Notes:
a. *The values shown above are an after tax reflection based on a tax rate of 20.00%.*
b. *Prior to age 59, a premature distribution tax is assessed to applicable accounts.*
c. *Any tax deferred or qualified accounts do not reflect any possible surrender charges.*
d. *Values shown are based on non-guaranteed interest rates shown above. Actual results will be different and may be more or less favorable.*

the only alternative that can deliver on *all* of these benefits at this magnitude for you.

Yes, you need to work hard to achieve millionaire status. You may start out with one property—your first home. But remember what the Thrivers of the world do? They repeat the process over and over again. They buy a second property, and then a third.

> **LINK TIP:** For a copy of the comprehensive plans of Liz, John, and Barry plus an audio/video explanation of them, go to the learning portal at www.MissedFortune.com/Millionaire-By-Thirty.

We promised to show you that by your thirties, your money can be earning as much or more than you do. Review Liz's illustration that we have created as a hypothetical example in figures 9.3 and 9.4, because it represents the potential that a successful asset optimization/equity management plan can deliver.

Please remember that you don't have to have hundreds or thousands of dollars in order to start one of these MFTA life insurance contracts that can become a phat CAT over time. You can create a maximum-funded, tax-advantaged life insurance policy with as little as $25 to $40 per month. The important thing is to assess and optimize what assets you do have—no matter how big or small—and start your plan now! You can increase your deposits and establish additional "buckets" as you begin to accumulate real estate equity that you will want to separate from your properties and invest safely as time goes on. Focus on what you want to end up with rather than the amount you have to begin with.

Asset optimization and successful equity management must contain several key ingredients to have it come together into a delightful treat. Envision a large banana split with three giant scoops of ice cream, each a different flavor. The three scoops of ice cream represent liquidity, safety, and rate of return—the real essence and purpose of the strategies we have laid out in this book. By repositioning serious cash into maximum-funded, tax-advantaged life insurance contracts, we have properly encompassed these three key elements of a prudent investment at its base. That's the banana that holds the serious cash. An added bonus to MFTA insurance is the income-tax-free life insurance death benefits that can be paid for with otherwise payable income tax when it is structured properly. It's like the whipped cream that covers the entire plan. The cherry on top of the sundae represents the tax-deductible interest that we may enjoy on some of the money we reposition as we become our own banker.

I ask, "Do you buy a banana split just for the cherry on top?" No. It's nice and it's attractive when it's there, but it is not essential for it to be a delicious treat to be savored and enjoyed. In other words, don't employ home equity management strategies contingent on having tax-deductible interest. I employ successful equity management primarily for liquidity, safety, and rate of return. If I get to deduct the interest on my tax return, it is simply the cherry on top that enhances my rate of return.

So, Does This Really Work in Real Life?

Adam: Hypothetical is okay, but what about in real life? Can I really do this?

Doug: You certainly can. In fact, a woman named Leticia actually did it faster than we've illustrated. When she started managing equity, she was in her late twenties and a single mother with three children. In the next five years she went from being a Striver (she bought a low-income HUD home[*] with no money down), all the way to being a Thriver. She accumulated a bunch of properties, more than a million dollars in her equity

---

[*] A home with financing from the government under the Department of Housing and Urban Development's program for low-income homebuyers. See http://www. hud.gov/buying/index.cfm#programs.

managment retirement plan, and a gorgeous house overlooking the Pacific near San Diego.

When we were in San Diego not long ago, Doug spent some time with Leticia, a smart, determined Latina woman who is now a professional mortgage planner. When she purchased her first house she was a single mother of three. She owned a tiny HUD home, financed under a program for low-income families. Then she lost her job.

In order to make money to feed her children, Leticia sold her HUD house for $17,000 more than she paid for it. She wondered if making such a handsome profit was illegal!

When she realized there was absolutely nothing illegal about selling real estate at a profit, she bought another house, sold it at a profit, and then did it again and again. After purchasing several houses, she said to herself, "I'm making more doing this than I made when I worked full-time." She taught friends how to do the same thing.

Fast-forward six years down the road. She and her new husband live in a beautiful house we visited near San Diego, and they have a vacation home in Hawaii. She owns a total of nine properties. She runs a busy mortgage company with three offices, and she has a net worth amounting to considerably more than $1 million.

This is not an isolated story. Many people have learned how to buy and sell properties, how to use positive leverage from real estate, and how to let compound interest work its magic, all while socking away money in nonqualified retirement savings plans. We should point out that it does take many hours and hard work to develop into the kind of Thriver that Leticia is. She had made this her full-time job.

The message here is that just as Leticia and others have done it, so can you. This is the millionaire mindset. It's not the "scarcity mentality" of Strivers who believe that others must fail in order for them to succeed, but the feast of abundance, as we first mentioned in chapter 2—where Thrivers see opportunities, not threats, all around them. Once you reach this stage, you can look forward to the myriad opportunities for the abundant future that life offers.

REMEMBER THIS

- Maximum-funded, tax-advantaged (MFTA) life insurance contracts are the only investment vehicles that accumulate money tax-free, allow you to access your money tax-free, and when you die your money blossoms in value and transfers income-tax-free.
- Properly structured, maximum-funded life insurance contracts can serve as the best retirement-planning, tax-sheltered vehicle available to Americans.
- A maximum-funded, tax-advantaged life insurance policy can become a "phat CAT" (Cash Accumulation Tool) that can make you financially independent by your thirties.
- Properly structured universal life insurance contracts are among those most conservative investments that pass the "LASER test" that you can choose to utilize for a worry-free retirement.
- Because of your age, you can be patient as your MFTA life insurance contracts accumulate money that can generate income that will last as long as you do. You can borrow rather than withdraw money from your policy so you can enjoy it in a tax-favored environment.
- An asset optimization/equity management plan can provide 50 percent more net spendable income, based on the same net income stream, when funded using MFTA life insurance as compared to traditional IRAs and 401(k)s that can potentially run out of money long before you and your spouse pass away.

LEARNING LINKS

Visit www.MissedFortune.com/Millionaire-By-Thirty and click on the learning portal for chapter 9 to:

- Study a set of sample plans and comparisons that show you how much better off you will be using MFTA life insurance as the core of your financial future savings plan.
- Gain more knowledge and background on insurance, plus read explanations of sections 72e, 7702, and 101(a) of the Internal Revenue Code, as well as how changes since the 1980s make MFTA insurance a great Cash Accumulation Tool.
- Read more about the tax code and the federal laws that govern the use of MFTA life insurance as explained in chapter 10 of *Missed Fortune 101,* chapter 17 of *Missed Fortune,* and Appendix A of *The Last Chance Millionaire.*
- Download a copy of the comprehensive plans of Liz, John, and Barry as illustrated in this chapter, plus listen to and view an audio/video explanation of each of the plans.
- Listen to an audio recording explaining the success formula for choosing the right investments, structuring your life insurance to perform as a superior investment, and accessing your money tax-free at retirement.
- Locate a properly trained professional from among our national network of financial experts in asset optimization and equity management.

CHAPTER 10

Touch All the Bases

Live a Life of Significance with Greater Clarity, Balance,
Focus, and Confidence

THERE IS A FAMOUS BASEBALL ANECDOTE about a Chicago
White Sox batter who hit a grand slam on opening day, but
when he failed to touch first base as he circled the bases, the umpire
ruled him out. The same is true with life: You need to touch all the
bases to be a winner.

You may think you have hit a home run because you have made
a lot of money, but the history books are filled with stories about
millionaires and billionaires who were miserable, despite their
wealth. They neglected their families; they cheated their customers; they did nothing philanthropic to pass along the message of
abundance.

In this chapter, Emron and Aaron will share from their perspec-
tives and experience to explore the importance of living a truly
wealthy life.

Wealth, What Does It Really Mean?

We believe it is important to live in a way that you balance all aspects of life—not just your financial wealth, but also your personal life, your relationships with your family, your dealings with others, and your commitment to society.

You are not going to fill your life with real significance until you optimize *all* your assets. We subscribe to the idea of a "family balance sheet" that reflects your life's entire assets: your core values; your experience; your civic, social, and religious contributions; and your monetary debits and credits.

On the chart below, you'll see how we judge "true wealth":

- *Financial assets*: This starts with the budget you have drawn up to live within your means; the properties you have bought to start on the road to equity management; plus the strategy of developing a future freedom and retirement plan that lasts into perpetuity, as we have outlined in the previous chapters.

- *Intellectual assets*: This category includes the knowledge you have gathered, along with the skills; ideas; reputation; alliances; good habits; and increasing wisdom you have acquired. You need to capture these assets so you can eventually share them with your spouse and children.

- *Civic assets*: This sector encompasses what you give back to society: your time, work, and means. It also includes the establishment of a family-empowered "bank" that can fund the charitable causes and societal goals your entire family embraces.

- *Core assets*: These are your personal and family values—your health standards; your unique abilities; your relationships; your heritage; and your spiritual beliefs that make the rest of a life of significance and abundance possible. Without solid core values, your life is incom-

FIGURE 10.1

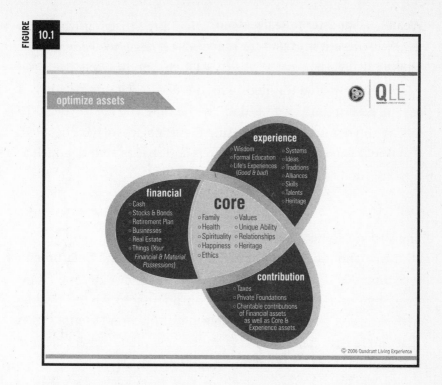

optimize assets

QLE

experience
- Wisdom
- Formal Education
- Life's Experiences (*Good & bad*)
- Systems
- Ideas
- Traditions
- Alliances
- Skills
- Talents
- Heritage

financial
- Cash
- Stocks & Bonds
- Retirement Plan
- Businesses
- Real Estate
- Things (*Your Financial & Material Possessions*)

core
- Family
- Health
- Spirituality
- Happiness
- Ethics
- Values
- Unique Ability
- Relationships
- Heritage

contribution
- Taxes
- Private Foundations
- Charitable contributions of Financial assets as well as Core & Experience assets.

© 2006 Quadrant Living Experience

plete. With them, your ideals can be passed along to future generations as your family grows.

I'm sure that like you, it's our upbringing that taught us the basic tenets above. The framework for grouping these values into a system of four main assets comes from Quadrant Living, which was developed by Lee Brower, president and founder of Empowered Wealth LC. Doug is an executive committee member and a founding architect of the Quadrant Living Experience, and he has adapted Lee's principles to fit with his outlook. We think it is crucial to create your own set of values that go beyond your finances, in order to make sure you stay in harmony with yourself, your family, and the world.

The point is that *life is not all about the money*. You can't get so focused on money that it becomes the only thing that matters. You can live a life that is much richer and more satisfying when you define your passions and your purpose. It is never too early in your adult years to start envisioning your life in a holistic way.

We have written this book with our dad, Doug, so that you can see the path to financial freedom by the time you are in your thirties. With your future secured using the strategies we have detailed, you'll find you can spread your wings and soar as an individual, as a spouse, and as a parent.

The Luckiest Generation?

More and more, our generation "wants to spend their time in meaningful and useful ways, no matter where they are," says *Time* magazine. As a group, we want to contribute to make our world a better place. A recent survey by the consulting firm Deloitte shows that "more than half of workers in their 20s prefer employment at companies that provide volunteer opportunities."[*]

Sometimes we don't realize just how lucky we are, coming of age in the early years of the twenty-first century. As young people, we have an optimistic vision of the future. Technology propels our life with new opportunities, from the Internet, to PDAs, to MP3s—with new inventions and the new ideas that accompany them, we seem able to dream bigger.

We already know that we want something more than to punch a time clock and get a paycheck, because we have seen that if people get into that rut, it destroys their spirit to dream and to achieve.

We are not cynical yet. We are still able to think, "What I want to do in life is to be compensated for the value that I bring. I can get involved in something larger than myself."

Of course, that is not true of everyone. Some of our peers are so selfish they have a hard time thinking of anything other than themselves or their immediate gratification. Others are scared of leaving

---

[*] Penelope Trunk, "What Gen Y Really Wants," *Time*, July 5, 2007.

the nest. Or their expectations have been disparaged or intimidated by parents who lost their jobs or were laid off by corporate America.

Thanks to the speed of communications, however, we are seeing more and more stories of "possibility thinkers"—people who see the glass as half full and want to help fill the remainder. "Being young could be a very selfish time of life," says Aaron, "but it's also a great opportunity. Since we don't yet have immediate family obligations or young children, many of us have discretionary time to devote to giving back."

We see examples of new attitudes among our generation every day.

There are professional athletes like Tiger Woods whom we admire because he seems to be a happy, loving father and husband. We admire the worldwide humanitarian efforts of movie stars like Angelina Jolie. When we were growing up, we loved basketball shoes, but our parents cringed at having to spend $150 for a pair— so we applaud NBA pro Stephon Marbury for putting his name on a sneaker that is affordably priced for all kids. Stephon inspired others: Ben Wallace of the Chicago Bulls signed on to the same affordable-sneaker endorsement deal not long ago.

As you might imagine, we're big fans of the Utah Jazz, yet the highlight of the 2007 playoffs for us was not the Jazz reaching the semifinals of the playoffs, but the off-court performance of Derek Fisher. When this star learned that his eleven-month-old daughter had a rare form of eye cancer, he decided that family came first. He actually skipped some of the playoff series in order to concentrate on finding the best care for her.

Family Vacations with a Purpose

Another step that helps define, capture, and grow a family's assets (and have fun!) is a "family vacation with a purpose."

Jennifer: I hear your whole family takes a vacation in Hawaii every other year. I love my folks, but I'd rather play and party if I were able to run away to Hawaii. Who wants to have their parents looking over their shoulder?

Emron: Our family works hard together, and we play hard together too. You should see how we compete in golf!! But we really love the time that we spend with our parents, our sisters, and their families. It's also a time to share what we've done during the previous year to enhance our assets.

Jennifer: I guess I'm skeptical. It sounds too much like school.

Emron: I know it might sound like that, but it's actually a cool feeling to reconnect with family and focus on goals together.

Each year, our family takes time out for a "family vacation with a purpose" that allows us to focus on the "big picture." These have been a tremendous help in summing up what we have done to enhance not just our financial health, but also our personal health, our relationships, and our civic and social accomplishments during the previous six months to a year.

When we go on our retreat in February to Maui, all family members are responsible for paying their own way. It's up to everyone to take off school and/or work in order to be there, because we do not want any empty chairs. Together we discuss more about how to create value, become self-reliant, and live life abundantly on a weeklong vacation. We've found we can learn more on a fun trip like this than the same time spent in school classes or even in what most workplaces can provide.

One year, our focus was to "consciously train the mind and body to unconsciously act in harmony with our family values and vision." This came from a book called *The Majesty of Calmness*, by William George Jordan. Our objectives were to develop leadership, become a high-impact family, discover our dynamic value, clarify who we are, learn to live in the proactive zone of predictable results, and understand how sharing is having more.

Now, don't get us wrong. We went scuba diving, biking, hiking, golfing, fishing, and did all kinds of activities. Yet what we remember most about these retreats is the time that we gathered together at breakfast and again in the evening for dinner to talk about enhancing all of our human, intellectual, financial, and civic assets.

In 2005, we decided that we would focus on our health and our family heritage. Our goal during this vacation was that we all would come away losing weight. So, we tried out an exercise program where we measured our steps by using Walk-o-meters every day. We disclosed the results on our Walk-o-meters and reset them in the evening before dinner. By increasing our motion several thousand steps a day and by cutting a couple hundred calories daily, we actually lost weight. We learned that by doing this over ninety days, a person can lose up to thirty pounds. And you should have seen how each of us strode in circles to boost our numbers!

In 2007, the theme was "to develop a master plan for a bigger future." We used a variety of inspirational ideas from such wonderful teachers as Dan Sullivan and his "Strategic Coach" program, Lee Brower and his Quadrant Living, and Marshall Thurber and his "Positive Deviants Network," which teaches how to succeed by embracing change rather than surrendering to conventional wisdom.

Before a recent summer mini-retreat, we all shared our goals and accomplishments. Emron and his wife, Harmony, announced that their "core assets" goals would include starting their own family. Emron talked about his "intellectual" goal to further develop software systems to help clients with their own financial futures. In the civic and social area, their contributions included supporting and participating in causes like the MS Walk for multiple sclerosis—something that is close to home because his sister-in-law suffers from the disease.

Meanwhile, Aaron reported that among his financial goals was closing on his new house and landscaping it, as well as preparing his new rental property for his first tenants. He also announced that he was ready to hit certain production goals at work. On the contribution side, he shared that after a friend's mother passed away from cancer, he had become very active in the American Cancer Society fund-raising drive called the Relay for Life.

The family also discussed another cause dear to our family's heart, the Ouelessebougou Alliance, a nonprofit organization that helps with vaccinations, education, water purification, schools, medicine, and economic opportunity in a small West African village in Mali. And both Emron and Aaron shared their experiences from actively volunteering in service opportunities at church.

Set Up Your Own Family-Empowered "Bank"

One thing we do on every full retreat is to explore how each of us can create value. There is always more opportunity in the universe than there is capability. It is often a matter of identifying a specific need in the world—particularly one that matches your passions—and finding a way to fill that need. Sometimes it can even come from trying to help people survive unfortunate events. If you remember in chapter 2, we described the people who answered a Y2K need with their seventy-two-hour emergency kits, and those have gone on to help people in all kinds of disasters.

We mentioned earlier that in the category of civic assets, every family can establish a family-empowered "bank." In our family, anyone can make contributions to our bank, or they can borrow from it. The idea is that just as with a real bank, we practice becoming our own bankers, so if a family member needs start-up money for a project, they can withdraw $20 to $2,000 to get started. But a family-empowered "bank" isn't just financial. You can deposit or borrow ideas, knowledge, experiences, and wisdom.

Jennifer: It sounds great that you have a family bank. I guess it's sort of a big piggy bank that you can empty when you need money for important things, right?

Aaron: That's not how we use it. First of all, we always must repay what we borrow. Second, I think the most important withdrawal I've made has been not money, but my dad's knowledge of financial planning and real estate. That's how both Emron and I have learned how to buy our first homes.

Emron: Down the line, I'm sure we will deposit much more in terms of our own experience—for example, the experience we have gained in writing this book. Hopefully we'll be able to "repay" our withdrawals with interest, sharing what we've learned from our own careers and philanthropic work.

A family-empowered bank can be a powerful force for your spouse, your parents, your cousins, and eventually your children. It's never just a handout—family members can take out loans for such things as additional schooling, but they pay them back with interest. Moreover, you can use its monetary assets to set up a formal family charitable foundation to make contributions to causes and charities that mean a lot to you.

LINK TIP: For details on how to set up a family-empowered "bank," visit www.MissedFortune.com/FamilyBank.

To us, sharing means having more. For example, we love riding all-terrain vehicles (ATVs), and we have donated three of them to our family bank so everyone in the family can enjoy them. We have also contributed snowmobiles, personal watercraft, condos, cabins, and timeshares. But sharing means being responsible and accountable. If anyone causes any damage to the material items in the bank, the user must be accountable and pay for the repairs.

How to Touch All the Bases Every Day and Wind Up Safe at Home

As young adults, we can benefit from the wisdom, experience, and knowledge of our parents. We can tap the knowledge of others inside or close to our family—people such as aunts, uncles, religious leaders, and neighbors—along with admirable historical figures. We can learn what daily living and professional strategies have worked for them, as well as what hasn't. When we find someone we want to emulate, we can ask them if they had the opportunity to do it again, how would they do it? Would they do something different? When we read about a noteworthy leader, we can ask ourselves how their lessons are applicable today.

It's important to keep life in perspective, too. As I'm sure you've found, pursuing talents and passions is important, but we can't let these kinds of activities rule our lives. Whether it's sports, arts, finances, or whatever, it's all just part of achieving a balance.

To use the baseball metaphor again, we can try to touch all the bases every day if possible, or at least every week—in terms of actions that lead to better outcomes. We can do this by meditating or praying or simply pondering how to enhance our core assets. Try to come up with three things you can do to make a symbolic deposit in your family "bank." It can be as simple as calling your mother or spouse to tell them you love them, or writing a thank-you note to somebody.

Here is a sample list of three things you could do daily or weekly:

Core Assets
- After a day of hard work, wind down by spending time with friends.
- Show appreciation or gratitude to someone from whom you have learned something useful.
- Exercise to maintain a healthful lifestyle.

Intellectual Assets

- Read a chapter from a book about your heritage, a heroic figure, or American history.
- Visit a historic site where you can learn from the struggles and achievements of others.
- Practice your skills or teach someone else how to read music or play an instrument.

Financial Assets

- Help a friend who has asked for financial advice how to balance their budget.
- Investigate a new real estate or investment venture.
- Hold a family financial council if expenditures are growing too fast or there has been a change in income.

Civic Assets

- Make a donation to a charity or cause you admire.
- Volunteer time to an event like the Race for the Cure, or to a place such as your local library.
- Have lunch or dinner with a civic leader whose efforts you appreciate and see what wisdom you can gain from his or her insights.

At first it may seem hard to come up with three new habits in each quadrant. But by setting up this system, you will get used to finding time for this important exercise in your daily life. And we guarantee the result: You'll grow as a person.

The "Blue Ocean" of Opportunities

To sum up, we hope you will join us in becoming "possibility think-ers." You can start right now today, to achieve great ideas such as:

- Being healthy and able to endure
- Sharing in the American dream and vision
- Becoming more entrepreneurial, thus enjoying freedoms of time, purpose, relationships, and money
- Enjoying what W. Chan Kim and Renee Mauborgne have called a "Blue Ocean" of opportunities that empower and intrigue as explained in their book, *Blue Ocean Strategy* (as opposed to a shark-infested "red ocean" characterized by a scarcity mentality).

As you become more financially secure, you will see that such opportunities are countless. There's not much of a limit on what you can do. Our generation showed its idealism when we helped people recover from Hurricane Katrina, and we will undoubtedly face new challenges, and face them well.

Thinking in terms of "abundance" rather than "scarcity," we know that something important awaits us beyond financial freedom. It is significance. We have an amazing chance to absorb the lessons from our parents' Baby Boomer generation—men and women who might have been stuck in a job they did not love or a house that became too confining for a growing family. We know that we want our lives to be worth more than a gold watch and a Social Security check.

We are past the industrial revolution. We are zooming through the information age. And we are moving ahead toward the conceptual age. As Daniel Pink explains in his book *A Whole New Mind*, to really excel in the twenty-first century, "high concept" needs to be coupled with "high touch."

That's why we have concluded with this chapter. After people want utility, they next desire significance. In a world of abundance, we can achieve things of great meaning that go way past a million-dollar net worth. That's a great goal, but most of all, we aim to leave behind a legacy.

We urge you to bask in abundance, to identify opportunities to contribute in every aspect of life, to grab the ball and run with it. By concentrating on optimizing all your assets, you can see through a wider, high-definition lens. Spend time each day adding value to your physical, mental, spiritual, financial, and social self.

When we talk with clients, we explain that the brilliant ideas embodied in Lee Brower's Quadrant Living Experience can be boiled down to these essential mental adjustments:

- Clarity
- Balance
- Focus
- Confidence

As you take control of your financial security, you will feel energized because of this new *clarity*. You can take the "wobble" out of your life with the proper *balance*. You will have greater accuracy in achieving goals and realizing your vision with the proper *focus*. Lastly, you will have increased *confidence* in all relationships—your spouse, children, employer, business associates, friends, faith, and money, which in turn will attract an endless supply of new opportunities.

So our final thought is to remind you not to limit your strategy to financial wealth alone. Touch all the bases, and you'll be a home-run leader in the game of life.

REMEMBER THIS

- True wealth is comprised of more than just financial assets. It involves human, intellectual, and contribution assets as well.
- Abundance breeds more abundance.
- The most important category on the family balance sheet is not the money; it's the human or core assets such as family, friends, health, values, spirituality, heritage, happiness, and your unique abilities.
- *Clarity* energizes people. *Balance* takes the wobble out of life and increases the velocity to achieve your goals quicker. *Focus* increases the accuracy in realizing your vision. And *confidence* attracts opportunities; lack of confidence repels opportunities.
- By holding regular family vacations with a purpose, you and your loved ones can have fun and also devote time to focus on optimizing all your assets.
- Consider establishing a family-empowered bank in which family members can borrow funds, obtain knowledge or help when needed, and also contribute to causes and charities you cherish.

LEARNING LINKS

Visit www.MissedForturne.com/Millionaire-By-Thirty and click on the learning portal for chapter 10 to:

- Download sample family retreat agendas and a template to help you plan and carry out your own family vacations with a purpose.
- Download a template to help you plan and get in the habit of touching all of the bases in the four quadrants on a daily, weekly, or monthly basis.

- Download how to establish a family bank and review a sampling of some of the experiences we have captured and deposited in our own family bank.
- Purchase a copy of *The Brower Quadrant* by Lee Brower, which provides wonderful insights into the Quadrant Living Experience.

Acknowledgments

An author's work can only be unique in the expression of ideas, which rarely, if ever, claim just one originator. Ideas are the result of countless interactions with people who influence the path one takes.

We wish to express sincere gratitude for the wonderful people who have helped and inspired us to create *Millionaire by Thirty*.

To our incredible literary agent, Jillian Manus, thank you for your excitement and encouragement in the creation of this work. You are so generous with your time and talents to help others. You have so much good in your heart, energy in your soul, and passion for life!

We give special thanks to our chief editor at Hachette Book Group USA, Mr. Rick Wolff, and his able assistant Tracy Martin, for a wonderful working relationship. You have believed in us and our message and the power of delivering it to the world. And thanks to all of the great people at Grand Central Publishing who have helped to make this book a success. Also thanks to Robert Castillo, managing editor at Hachette Book Group USA, and your team of editors for your great work.

To our mother and wife, a loving companion of more than thirty-four years, thank you for your love, compassion, patience, and understanding as we pursue those things about which we are passionate. You have been by our side rendering assistance and encouragement with every project we have undertaken. We love you dearly!

As sons, we offer gratitude to our father, hero, and mentor, for the opportunity and experience to work on this project together. We would never be where we are today without your faith, confidence, and example. Thank you for the opportunity to pass on and share what you and Mom have taught us. We look forward to working on many more projects together.

As a father, I express gratitude to my sons, Emron and Aaron, for the wonderful inspiration and contributions you both made to this work. Special thanks for helping with all of the charts and graphs, as well as the case studies in this work. I feel so fortunate and blessed to be your father.

Special thanks to our entire family, especially to my daughters and our sisters, Mailee, Adrea, Mindy, and Ashley, for all of your help and support in our mutual endeavors. Thanks to Harmony, my (Emron's) wife, for your constant love and support, especially during this project while being pregnant with our first son, Ethan. Thanks also to Scott and Brian, my sons-in-law/brothers-in-law, for your incredible talents and help in our business development. Our greatest love and joy is found in our family.

Thanks to Grace Lichtenstein for her help in organizing this work. Grace, it was a delight to work with you closely throughout this project as you helped capture so many of the ideas and expressions from all three of us. Thanks for holding us to the task at hand.

We are grateful for Heather Beers, a wonderful friend and editor. We sincerely appreciate your special talents and your encouragement. We also extend special thanks to Toni Lock at tmdesigns for her help with the layout of the charts, graphs, and illustrations in this work. We express sincere gratitude to Kristin Varner for her unique and professional artwork. Amid your busy schedules, you all came through beautifully using your incredible talents.

We express special appreciation to Marshall Thurber and Lee

Brower for your encouragement, inspiration, and advice, which have contributed to the successful completion of this book.

Many teachers and mentors have influenced our lives. Thanks to our coaches: Dan Sullivan, Lee Brower, Adrienne Duffy, and Leo Weidner. Thanks to Don Blanton, John Childers, Mike Midlam, Marv Neumann, Philip Bodine, Jerry Davis, Philip Tirone, and Bill Sefton for the brainstorming and ideas that we have shared, created, and enhanced together.

We express gratitude to our talented and dedicated unique ability team for the countless hours of help and assistance you all render in our mutual endeavors.

Finally, we feel overwhelmingly thankful for our TEAM network of professional financial advisors, especially our core group of Missed Fortune Associates and Missed Fortune Producer Group. Thanks to Bill Sefton for your banana split metaphor and to Chuck Oliver for inspiring the Lifetime Learning Commitment (LLC). Also thanks to our many alliances, particularly Bill Zimmerman and your team, who have invested time, energy, and money in supporting the Missed Fortune Producer Group in helping people optimize their assets, manage their equity, and empower their true wealth. Together we are better—and we can turn this world right side up!

Index

For more information about these concepts . . .

If you would like to explore and possibly implement strategies contained in this book but are not sure how to do so, please seek advice from a financial professional.

If this book was given or recommended to you by a financial professional, you may choose to seek his or her advice, as well as advice from your personal tax advisor.

If you prefer, we can refer you to a professional trained in the strategies contained in this book. This network of financial professionals is referred to as The Equity Alliance Matrix (TEAM). If you would like to contact or be contacted by a TEAM member, please phone the Missed Fortune™ home office toll free at 1-888-987-5665, e-mail them at info@MissedFortune.com, or contact them through their Web site by visiting www.MissedFortune.com. If you are a financial services professional, insurance specialist, mortgage specialist, CPA, tax attorney, or real estate agent and would like information on how to qualify to become a member of TEAM and Missed Fortune Associates, please contact them in the same manner.

The authors, Douglas, Emron, and Aaron Andrew, are nationally recognized speakers and teach the Missed Fortune True Wealth Transformation™ strategies in public seminars throughout America, as well as through TeleSeminars and Webinars. For dates and times of these presentations that are conducted regularly, visit www. MissedFortune.com/Seminars.

For additional insights, please refer to Douglas R. Andrew's other works, *Missed Fortune, Missed Fortune 101*, and *The Last Chance Millionaire*.